PROFESSIONAL BALANCE

The Careerstyle Approach to Balanced Achievement

RICK GRIGGS

Griggs ACHIEVEMENT/Manfit Press
P.O. Box 2390
San Ramon, CA 94583
1-888-647-4447
www.griggsachieve.com

Professional Balance
The Careerstyle Approach to Balanced Achievement
Rick Griggs

Library of Congress Cataloging-in-Publication Data

Griggs, Rick, 1955–
    Professional Balance.

    Bibliography: p.
    1. Success—Psychological aspects. 2. Success in business—Psychological aspects. 3. Life Style.
I. Title.
BF637.S8G696   1989   646.7   89-12520
ISBN   0-922530-00-9

Printed in the United States of America

10 9 8 7 6 5 4 3

Associate Publisher: Maureen Biro
Production coordination and editing: Elaine Fritz & Associates
Design and typography: The Printed Page
Cover design: California Design Group

For information on seminars and consulting services offered by
Griggs ACHIEVEMENT, call or write:

Rick Griggs, President
Griggs ACHIEVEMENT/Manfit Press
P.O. Box 2390
San Ramon, CA 94583
1-888-647-4447

www.griggsachieve.com

DEDICATION

This book is dedicated to the three people who made it possible for me to continue building a business and to write about Professional Balance. . .

Dr. Reginald Griggs, Ron Griggs, and Marybeth Tahar

ACKNOWLEDGMENTS

Many thank-yous go to Sharon Morash, Dorothy Montgomery, Laura Pianka, Linda Jackson, Mike Elsesser, and Ed Barrett for their encouragement and the recognition that my ideas needed to be publicized. The hard work and dedicated effort of Elaine Fritz, Lila Aminian, and Maria Mancini in producing the book was valuable and much appreciated.

Special thanks to Christine Pedersen for providing computer support in the initial stages and moral support in the form of kicks in the pants during the latter stages of writing, and to Dr. Gary Silver for setting me straight on cardiac health and physiology.

A final note of admiration goes to my clients and customers for recognizing that balanced management training and personal development combine to make strong individuals and a powerful workforce.

CONTENTS

Preface   vii

1   What Is Professional Balance?   1

2   Exercise for Success (Or Until You Laugh)   11

3   Nutrition and Weight Control   25

4   Ten Achievement Factors   39

5   Women: Climbing, Grasping, and Gasping   55

6   Men and the "Little-Big Boy Syndrome"   71

7   Sex and Professional Balance   85

8   The Heart of Achievement   101

9   What to Do About Stress   115

10   Success with People   137

11   To Fail or Not to Fail   153

12   Setting the Right Kinds of Goals   167

13   The Psychology of Achievement   181

14   Conclusion   195

Appendix: 100 Ways to Control Stress and Nurture Success   199

PREFACE

After spending several years researching, writing, testing, and rewriting this book, I still vividly recall my original intent in publishing *Professional Balance.* I had just finished teaching a course to a group of business owners. They were pleased that we had included tips and techniques that touched on both their professional and personal lives. One woman remarked, "You should write a book—of all the books I've read, this would be the most useful." I was disturbed by the suggestion, because all of my time and efforts were going into establishing and growing my business. The last thing I needed was to go off on another quixotic chase that I knew would take a lot of time.

I thought about it, procrastinated, and then decided to do a bit of test marketing. I put together the initial chapters in a booklet with the original title of *Careerstyle: How to Balance Your Personal and Professional Lives.* With very little editing or investment in packaging, the darn things kept selling out after classes, speeches, or management retreats. It convinced me that it would be worth investing the time and energy needed to complete the book. Maybe I wouldn't be chasing windmills after all.

This book is for professionals. They may be soon-to-be professionals, professionals in practice, training to be professionals in some chosen field, or simply people with the intention of entering a specific field or industry. Any achiever who paces the halls during the day or lies awake at night mulling over ideas for getting a real competitive edge in life will find the tools they need in these pages. It is meant to be a handbook that can be used over and over again during the search for equilibrium in life.

It's painful to see someone's years of education and study blossom into promising career opportunities and financial success, only to watch that career start to unravel in some nook or cranny of life. These hidden corners of our lifestyle are the areas we don't think are very important. Or maybe we know they're important, but we just can't find the time or energy to take care of them. The saying about how the chain is only as strong as its weakest link is very true. Over and over I've heard people say: *If only I had watched my weight...managed my success...learned from failure...or exercised more, I wouldn't have burned out...given up...or lost it all.* I've also seen it at the organizational level in various industries, factories, and workforces: Good quality, great products, and innovative services are sometimes wasted because of a few weak links, Band-Aid patch jobs, or the sudden loss of a key person. These individual and organizational tragedies are my greatest motivation in writing this book.

Our Griggs ACHIEVEMENT seminars, workshops, and management retreats have been filled with the information in this book. The idea of balance is a key concept when we teach time management to bank managers. Balance applies when we take 15 vice-presidents through our public speaking program. Every time we implement a quality improvement program at a high technology company, the principles of Professional Balance make the program more complete and effective. A lot of time and dollars are spent on remedial, basic, and advanced job training at all levels, but the future may depend more on a balanced approach and balanced people than on specific skills. We are committed to teaching basic skills, advanced techniques, and balance in all things.

This is a positive book for positive people. Read it if you truly believe in the power to change. If you are firmly convinced that you can change your habits, thoughts, and understanding, this book will tell you how. If you're not sure you can, it'll make you sure. The ideas you are about to study have been tested and refined in many different settings and a variety of circumstances. People appreciate good, solid information that can positively affect their lives. *Professional Balance* gives you the information you need to succeed at work, at home, and in life. Read it twice.

Rick Griggs
Mountain View, California
April, 1989

1

WHAT IS
PROFESSIONAL BALANCE

Professional balance is a set of principles that people can use to put their lives in order. It's a healthy mix of planning and analysis that allows you to balance all the things you need to do today in such a way that you will be fully satisfied with your achievement throughout your entire life. The way you manage your work, health, goals, sex life, and stress level determines how balanced you are and how successful you will be.

This book will cover a lot of ground. Some chapters will be a review of what you already know, while others explore brand-new territory. Search for the big picture on every page and in every paragraph. Review familiar material and re-read some of the new. It all fits together to create balance in your life—not only today but ten, twenty, or even sixty years from now. Use this text as a handbook for your personal achievement in anything you choose.

Men and women often find that their road to success has taken a detour. The tricks, myths, and hot tips about how to achieve bliss are futile. You may have tried following the advice you read in magazines or hear on TV talk shows, but something always seems to be missing. What's missing is a balanced foundation. This book doesn't offer you tricks or fads.
It gives you the basics.

We're going to emphasize a combination of good career strategy, personal development, and fitness. If you prefer, call it a balance between career and health, or between the professional and personal parts of your life. Most of us keep these two sides of our lives separate, which results in immeasurable stress, waste, and confusion. If this

1

book gives you just one idea to smooth the interface between your two lives, it will be well worth your time and money. It's clear that the two must go hand in hand if you are to succeed over the long run.

We're going to use the word *Careerstyle* to describe this balanced approach, which allows you not only to succeed, but also to have some power and joy in your professional and personal life. Careerstyle includes the basics, like what you need to know to exercise correctly, the importance of eating good food, and how to take care of your heart. It includes successfully dealing with the changing roles of men and women, both in business and at home, and recognizes the role of your sex life in your career success. It includes learning to use your failures to actually achieve more, how to set goals, and the psychology of accomplishment.

Women have unique priorities and desperately need a balanced focus for their new roles. There is no doubt that, all things being equal, women can accomplish just as much as men. The problem is that they may wear themselves out trying to emulate a model that hasn't worked very well for men, and certainly won't work for women.

Women are not alone in suffering from society's expectations. We also see men who are stuck in what I call the "Little-Big Boy Syndrome." Men are often forced to be big boys long before they're ready. This results in emotional limitations that can ruin both careers and love relationships. Whereas women are casting off old roles and plunging into new ones, men have a lot of unlearning to do. The theme of this book is that men and women in any profession or career can fulfill their aspirations in a positive and satisfying way. The balance of Careerstyle guarantees it.

Building our lives and ambitions on foundations that aren't balanced and solid is like building a castle on a three-legged foundation. We use the excuse that we're working so hard on the castle that we don't have time to finish that last leg. We plan to get it done as soon as we finish the next turret and have some breathing space. The problem is that too often, when we finish that turret on our "achievement castle," the pressure to get the next one done is greater than the pressure to finish leg number four of the foundation. This book is about completing leg number four, or three, or even two and putting together a solid, balanced foundation for achievement.

One part of a balanced Careerstyle that many people fail to develop is their physical fitness. The traditional approach of persuading people to take better care of their bodies has not worked. People either quit after several weeks or they push too hard, too fast, and end up dying too soon. High achievement in business, career, health, or athletics requires a well-thought-out plan of action that includes taking excellent care of the mind, the career, and the body at the same time.

A successful strategic life plan may require some short-term sacrifice. As a young boy, I desperately wanted a ten-speed bicycle. My mother agreed to pay the first half if I could earn the second half. With that shiny bicycle in mind, my brother and I spent many Saturdays going door to door painting addresses on curbs for a dollar. We missed some great water fights, BB gun wars, and asphalt football games, but we had the best ten-speeds on the block.

I've personally had many low moments when I felt I was wasting my time and that I was the only idiot doggedly pursuing a set path. People around me advised me to relax, let it go, and have a little more fun in life. My gut feeling, however, was that I had to continue to concentrate on my goals and plan for reaching them in order to relax and have more fun throughout my life. The key was that the activity fit into the strategic plan. The plan may have been a bit blurry sometimes, but I could see that my long-term satisfaction would more than make up for the dog days. Does anyone know how many exciting BB gun wars equal a new bicycle?

Everything needs to be evaluated for costs and benefits. Business professionals are paid to get the most out of every dollar spent. Any activity that does not serve a specific need or service is quickly terminated in most well-run organizations. A well-run personal career can't afford to be any less rigorous. Everything you do should be evaluated for its effectiveness in getting you closer to the general plan for your life.

Life is made up of small decisions. A good example is what approach we take in caring for our bodies. There is a lot of advice available. Some people preach that a grand scheme of exercise, diet, pills, and equipment will save you, while others pound their fists and say that this fanatical type of plan will kill you. Good personal development programs fall somewhere between these two extremes.

Many businesses support the fitness movement. They cannot close their eyes to the astounding statistics on the high cost of poor health and the money-saving advantages of good fitness programs. About 1.5 million Americans suffer heart attacks each year, and a third of them do not live to talk about it. Industry pays over $700 million a year to replace these victims.

When it comes to nutrition, even the celebrities are catching on. Johnny Carson's second wife Joanna said that better eating habits would have kept their marriage together. Sophia Loren says that she always eats three meals a day and quits while she's still a little hungry.

On the other hand, many still believe that exercise and nutrition programs are a waste of time and money. Unfortunately, well-documented disasters give these folks plenty of ammunition. Many professionals normally trained to make critical and logical decisions confuse some of the propaganda with the facts. People cite the case of a well-known runner/writer who died of a heart attack while jogging. Some statistics (out of context) say that those who exercise are five times more likely to have a heart attack while exercising. The complete story is that inconsistent exercise activity (the weekend warrior) increases the likelihood of heart attack considerably, while consistent exercise reduces the overall risk.

You may know some anti-exercise friend who points out that it takes dozens of miles to burn off a milkshake and you'll probably get hit by a car or get cancer from exhaust fumes. This book is for professionals who are skilled at separating logical arguments from excuses.

A one-sided lifestyle that excludes either career development strategies or health and personal improvement strategies will never be successful in the full sense of the term. Both require the same conscious decision making. Consider the times when you are at your professional best. You have the facts on an issue, you've analyzed alternatives, and are ready to choose and implement your selection. How many times do you apply these top-notch decision-making skills to your entire lifestyle?

Your career training has taught you to distinguish between the right and wrong ways of doing what you do. You have probably spent a lot of time, energy, and hard-earned money to train yourself in specific skill areas. With the experience you've acquired in addition to your training, you make decisions and judgment calls almost without thinking. You could probably teach someone else the process you go through almost instinctively. The same principles and skills can be used to make your personal development activities more successful. The leverage you'll get from managing the personal side of your life as consciously as your professional life will pay off with incredible leverage for long-term success.

Running your business or professional career and running your health and fitness lifestyle have a lot in common. The chapter on exercise goes into a lot of detail on making physical fitness a workable part of your routine. The Achievement Factors chapter covers many of the business principles used by the brightest business professionals in the country.

Even your sex life has influence over your professional and personal success. Because sex, like food, water, and air, is one of the primary human drives, its presence (or lack of it) is bound to have an affect on your overall achievement. The section on sex is not just thrown in to spice up your reading or to sell more books, but to show that equilibrium in the major aspects of our lives is a must. A cross-country trip by car needs an engine that's tuned, a cooling system that works, clear fuel lines, and safe tires. A problem in any area could cut the trip short in the middle of New Mexico at 2:00 a.m.

There is a proposition in economics called the "Theory of the Firm," based on the definition of business as an enterprise that delivers products and services in accordance with prevailing supply and demand conditions in the marketplace. To succeed, the firm's products and services must fill a definite consumer need. Measurements of business performance usually include quality, on-time delivery, and fair and reasonable prices. A separate measure for service is often added. The Careerstyle concept provides a parallel approach to the management of your life—a firm must perform well in many interrelated areas, and the same applies to your life. You can produce great results if you pay attention to all the parts of your life.

There is a great cost to paying attention to one part of your life at the expense of another. For example, the woman who puts her professional career above her physical fitness has already built a major barrier into her career path. More and more executives are convinced that the same qualities that lead to success and promotability in business are found in those who continually persist in their health programs. Those who are balanced regularly outperform those without a solid foundation.

Business is longing to find men and women who can endure pain, discouragement, and setbacks, only to get back up and continue a program that will lead to better mental and physical well-being. When you consider that companies also get the benefits of reduced medical costs, lower absenteeism, and higher productivity, it's easy to see that employees like this have that superior potential that human resources departments dream of finding.

On the other hand, it's possible to spend a lot of time and money on your fitness program without getting a reasonable return on your investment. The man who lives in the weight room and goes about his limited fitness program the same way month after month is only getting 50 cents on his fitness dollar. A one-sided fitness program like this may lead to great muscle development, but he'll miss out on the vitality and well-being that comes from a balanced routine. This guy needs to leverage workable business techniques to get full fitness value.

Consider the champions of the last Olympics, or Wimbledon: can anyone believe that they won medals and trophies because they simply tried harder? Not at all. True champions continue to win because they first learn all available techniques and then apply them to specific areas for improvement. The Careerstyle guidelines in this book will teach you how to multiply your chances of success by developing both personal and professional skills in tandem.

Careerstyle implies that we bear the risk (in the economic sense of the word) of personal development just like we bear the risk of competing in the professional business world. In both business and personal development, all opportunities should be maximized, leveraged, and fully developed. On the negative side, the possibility of business failure, job loss, physical injury, or even death should be understood and minimized.

Professional athletes need coaches along the way to meet their goals, and Careerstyle insists that successful people must make use of professional expertise to enhance personal development. There is amazing leverage available to you if you get access to the coaching of people who are masters in areas you are in the process of developing.

This book is for the truly successful 5–7% of the population who are determined to make the most of their professional, personal, and physical potential. The challenge is to take charge now, use your good business sense in planning and executing your strategy, and play to your strengths. We live business everyday: we set goals, we monitor progress, and we make corrections. You're going to learn through reading this book how to use that approach to increase your personal achievement levels, put yourself on a high level of fitness and well-being, and manage your stress level so that you can live long enough to spend all the money you're going to earn.

FOR FURTHER READING

Borysenko, Joan. *Minding the Body, Mending the Mind.* New York: Bantam Books, 1988.

Felder, Leonard. *How to Let Go of Emotional Baggage and Enjoy Your Life Again.* New York: New American Library, 1987.

Frankl, Viktor. *Man's Search for Meaning.* New York: Simon & Schuster, 1984.

Hill, Napoleon. *Think and Grow Rich.* New York: Ballantine Books, 1960.

Johnson, Spencer. *The Precious Present.* New York: Doubleday, 1984.

POINTS TO REMEMBER/THINGS TO DO

1. Your balance will affect your success.
2. Today's activities will combine for tomorrow's results.
3. The highest achievers take time for themselves.
4. Read about successful men and women in history.
5. Follow the lives of successful people still living.
6. Skim the remaining 12 chapters of the book.
7. Go directly to the chapters that interest you.
8. Read all chapters within four weeks.

MY BALANCED ACHIEVEMENT INVENTORY
How Many Bases Do You Get For Balance?

YOUR LIFE!

WRITTEN GOALS = 1ST BASE

WRITTEN GOALS + MODERATE EXERCISE = 2ND BASE

WRITTEN GOALS + MODERATE EXERCISE + GOOD EATING = 3RD BASE

WRITTEN GOALS + MODERATE EXERCISE + GOOD EATING + ACHIEVEMENT FACTORS = HOME RUN!

WRITTEN GOALS + MODERATE EXERCISE + GOOD EATING + ACHIEVEMENT FACTORS + STRESS MANAGEMENT = 2 RUNS!

WRITTEN GOALS + MODERATE EXERCISE + GOOD EATING + ACHIEVEMENT FACTORS + STRESS MANAGEMENT + LOVE + ROMANCE = 3 RUNS!

WRITTEN GOALS + MODERATE EXERCISE + GOOD EATING + ACHIEVEMENT FACTORS + STRESS MANAGEMENT + LOVE + ROMANCE + FAILURE CONTROL = GRAND SLAM

2

EXERCISE FOR SUCCESS
(Or Until You Laugh)

My first exercise program was a direct result of my first entrepreneurial efforts. When my brother and I were kids, we went into business selling avocados in front of the entrance to the largest supermarket in our neighborhood, offering customers a 60% savings compared to the avocados inside. Unfortunately, the avocados were stolen from a local orchard, so Sergeant Hayes from the police station put an end to our ambitions to join the Fortune 500. The Sergeant took us to the station and told us that our father was taking time off work to come talk to him, which made us shake in our boots, but he also told us that we were good boys and smart, too! The problem was that we had too much free time and energy. All this was building up to enrolling us in his judo class, where we learned about fitness, self-defense, and other life skills. That physical activity turned out to be a turning point in our lives. From then on we legally painted addresses on curbs for $1 a house!

Exercise can conjure up extreme images of pain and boredom or the ecstasy of orgasmic relief. To some people the word exercise means painful plodding, while to others the same word means thrilling excitement. In the context of your Careerstyle, exercise is one of the building blocks to a satisfying life.

Napoleon Hill in his Law of Success writes that "Physical endurance is one of the most essential factors in achieving success." Teddy Roosevelt traveled into the Dakota Badlands with Buffalo Bill Cody mainly because he knew that to reach his high goals he had to have a rugged constitution and be in superb health.

This chapter is designed to show you the powerful effect that exercise can have on your sense of well-being and pleasure in your life, which in turn contributes to your personal success. We'll also look at the best ways of exercising so that you reach your peak performance—neither over- nor under-stressing your body. We'll deal with how to set up an exercise program that's fun and exhilarating, not a grind-it-out-because-it's-good-for-me project.

COURAGE, CONFIDENCE, AND BENEFITS

Speaking of benefits, this field is full of them. Proper exercise builds a confident attitude that will be noticed in everything that you do. People who are fit tend to take the bull by the horns when necessary. They have few problems with being assertive at appropriate times. They know that their bodies are strong and healthy, so they have extra courage and endurance that translate into a phenomenal competitive edge.

Two primary human drives—food and sex—benefit directly from good exercise. You probably know people that avoid exercise on the basis that it doesn't burn enough calories to make up for being hungrier afterward. However, exercise actually changes your metabolism so that you burn more calories 24 hours a day, even when sitting quietly! Some people find that exercise actually suppresses their appetites.

Other people who prefer the life of a couch potato say that exercise makes you too tired to have a good sex life. Bull! Research proves them wrong over and over. A fit body is less likely to experience headaches and lethargy when it's time for romance!

EXCITING RESEARCH

The latest findings in exercise physiology point to some interesting trends. Exercise can be more effective than sophisticated pharmacological treatments. For example, thrombolytic therapy deals with dissolving potentially fatal blood clots. Two of the thrombolytic drugs, streptokinase and urokinase, have been actively studied since 1968 for heart attack prevention. The two major considerations are that streptokinase causes bleeding and urokinase is expensive. Researchers know that tissue-type plasminogen activator (t-PA) is a protein that has a positive effect on blood clots without the negative side effects. Developing enough t-PA is the problem, but researchers have found that exercise can release t-PA from the cells in one's body.

In this day of AIDS and other disorders of the body's immune system, scientists around the globe are frantically digging for breakthroughs. A promising note is that some studies find that moderate and consistent exercise actually strengthens the immune system.

EXPERIMENT UNTIL YOU LAUGH

I'm going to make a statement that may surprise you: If your exercise program isn't fun, it's useless. That sounds a bit extreme, and you may have a belief that something that's good for you involves struggle and discipline, but remember we're talking about your lifetime of achievement. Psychologists know that if an activity isn't in some way rewarding, it will be discontinued. (We'll discuss this concept in detail in Chapter 13.) Human beings aren't designed to keep up a behavior that doesn't produce some short-term pleasures.

I recommend that you find several activities that stand up to the criteria for fitness programs that are outlined later in this chapter. Start doing the ones that you like the most. Set up your program so that the chances of your having fun are high. The more you laugh, the better. If the activity makes you grin from ear to ear as you get better at it, you've got a good one!

I used to teach an adult women's gymnastics class in Palo Alto, California. Their skills and motivation seemed to be much higher than that of the average health/fitness enthusiast, so I thought it would be interesting to ask what motivated them to come to the gym month after month, year after year. Here are some of their revealing comments:

"It's fun...plain and simple. It's fun."

"Accomplishment...I can accomplish things here that my body never used to be able to do."

"I enjoy progressively achieving higher and higher goals."

"I look and feel ten years younger."

"I love the thrill of learning new and exciting things with my body."

"It's an ego boost for people to tell us we have great bodies."

"The mental and physical boost is tremendous."

Even though I'd been teaching the class for years, I had not realized that fun and the thrill were just as important as the exercising itself. These women continued over the years because their exercise program produced fun, achievement, and excitement in their lives.

By the way, I've kept tabs on the career progress of some of these healthy ladies. At this writing they are rapidly moving up in some of the most well-respected and fastest growing firms in America. Some are getting Ph.Ds at Stanford University in addition to their full-time work. Others travel nationwide marketing state-of-the-art computer workstations or do pioneering work in artificial intelligence. They may have come to class tired, even exhausted, but they continued to create time for their personal health and fitness. You can follow their lead and make some wise additions to your lifestyle.

THE MAGIC FORMULA

The "magic formula" according to exercise physiologists is that you need to exercise three to five times each week, and that you must keep your heart rate within your training zone for at least 15 minutes each time (more on this later). You're a professional person in your career, so you'll understand that like any skill, exercise is not a haphazard affair. The formula must be followed or there will be no positive effect, or worse yet, you could kill yourself.

We have too many examples of injuries, heart attacks, and sudden deaths associated with exercise. This should motivate you to understand the basics of exercise—remember that if you remain sedentary, you also put your life in danger. The fact that you are reading this chapter suggests that you have the motivation to learn about good exercise habits.

Getting your physician involved is a must. Some say that if you are reasonably healthy and if you start an exercise program slowly, you should have no problems, and they're probably right. But, as we learned with Jim Fixx, Arthur Ashe, and John Kelley (Grace's brother)—athletes in apparently superb health who suffered heart attacks—it is possible to have a medical problem that doesn't show. It's worth getting checked out.

Choose a doctor that has respect for your goals. If you are unfortunate enough to run into a physician that doesn't listen to your health concerns, appears too busy to pay attention, and seems to find quick chemical solutions rather than working with you on a balanced fitness program, get out and find another doctor who is oriented toward prevention and balance. There are plenty of good physicians who believe in balanced, long-term programs.

YOUR TRAINING ZONE

If exercise is going to do you any good, it must be of a certain intensity. The sticky part is that the required intensity is different for each person, for different ages, and for various states of health. Your body has a built-in barometer—your heart rate—that tells you just how well you're doing. If you choose to listen, it will tell you when you're doing too much and when it's not enough.

Your heart rate indicates how well your cardiovascular system is handling the stress being placed on it. Your training (or target) zone is the range of heart beats per minute at which you get good fitness results without overdoing it.

To arrive at your training zone, start by subtracting your age from the number 220. A 35-year-old would arrive at the number 185 (220 -35 = 185). This is the average maximum heart rate for a 35-year-old. In other words, this person's heart rarely beats faster than 185 times a minute. From this number, calculate 60% and 80% for the low and high ends of the target zone: 220 - 35 = 185; 185 X 0.60 = 111, and 185 X 0.80 = 148. The training zone for a 35-year-old is 111 bpm to 148 bpm (bpm = beats per minute). Our 35-year-old should get his or her heart rate up to 111 bpm three to five times a week for 15 to 30 minutes, and should be careful not to go over 148 bpm. By the way, a person's maximum heart rate drops by about one beat every year.

SLOW DEATH VS. SUDDEN DEATH

Fainting, profuse sweating, jitters, heart attacks, and sudden death can result when people go above the top end of their training zone. A rule of thumb is that you should be able to carry on a light conversation while you are exercising. If you can't talk, slow down, because you've probably gone over the top of your training zone and entered the sudden death zone.

On the other hand, if you stay below the bottom end of your training zone (60%), you are in the slow death zone. If you spend your life in the slow death zone, the finale may not be as dramatic, but you will be just as dead as the weekend heros who keep overshooting the ceiling of their training zones.

Slow Death. The last time Mark exercised was about twenty years ago when he was in high school. He hated it then, and doesn't dare try it now. Besides, his golfing, bowling, and walking to meetings all day long give him all the exercise he needs, according to him. In reality, Mark is slowly choking off his vitality and energy, and the efficiency of his cardiovascular and immune systems are slowly deteriorating.

His attitude may kill him. He's definitely entering the slow death zone.

Sudden Death. Joanne is 36, smokes continuously, drinks a fair amount, and can barely handle her high-stress job. To make up for her lifestyle, she attends a vigorous aerobics class once a week. She sometimes misses her class if she's traveling or if she's too exhausted to go. She doesn't know it, but during class her heart rate soars to about 97% of her maximum (178 bpm). If she keeps this up, stress may no longer be a problem, because Joanne is in the sudden death zone.

TAKING YOUR PULSE

Here's some information on how to properly take your pulse. The two most common locations for taking your pulse are on the thumb side of the wrist (radial pulse) and the side of the throat (carotid pulse). Others include the femoral pulse on the inside of the thigh, the temporal pulse on the temple, and for those with pronounced heart beats, the 10-finger pulse (all ten fingers touching at the tips). Your exercise pulse should be taken for 6 seconds and multiplied by 10 (# X 10 = beats per minute). Another option is to take a 15-second pulse and then multiply by 4 (# X 4 = bpm).

An exercise pulse taken for longer that 15 seconds will be inaccurate, because the heart begins to slow down from the moment you stop the activity to take your pulse. The first six seconds give the best picture of what your heart was doing while you were actually exercising.

FIVE FITNESS COMPONENTS

To be in peak condition, you need to be fit in five areas: muscle strength, muscle endurance, flexibility, cardiovascular efficiency, and bodyfat percentage.

Muscle strength is the force of a single contraction. An excellent example is that of the weight lifter who with one swift movement lifts the entire weight from the chest and shoulders up to an extended position above the head. The old-fashioned view of fitness centered solely on muscle strength. Muscle endurance involves the repeated action of a group of muscles over time. Examples include light weight lifting, rowing, lifting several boxes onto shelves, or some portions of aerobics classes (usually floor work).

Flexibility focuses on the range of motion in the joints, muscles, tendons, and ligaments. The flexible gymnast usually comes to mind, but many football and basketball teams are using flexibility trainers to reduce injuries and to speed up recovery time. Flexible bodies get hurt less often and heal much more quickly when they do suffer an injury.

Cardiovascular efficiency, also known as circulo-respiratory efficiency, refers to the efficient exchange of fresh oxygen for carbon dioxide and other waste gases and products. The hearts, lungs, and blood vessels of fit and healthy individuals can make this exchange without much effort. This means that for a given amount of activity such as stair climbing, cardiovascularly fit people will pant less and their heart rates will not rise as much. Even when they're at rest, their pulse rates on the average will be lower than those of a twin brother, sister, or office mate who does not exercise.

Bodyfat percentage refers to the percentage of overall bodyfat in relation to lean body mass. This component of complete physical fitness, like your pulse rate, is another barometer of fitness. Healthy ranges for men are from about 15–18%, and for women are from 20–23%. If you diet without exercising, there is a risk of losing muscle instead of fat. Muscle is denser and weighs more than fat, so if you reduce calorie intake without exercising, you may lose weight in the form of muscle tissue, while still maintaining an unhealthy percentage of fat.

WHAT'S A GOOD WORKOUT?

A good workout has five parts: preparation, warm-up, training phase, cool-down, and acknowledgment.

Preparation. Although excercise is important there's no need to make a big production of preparing for it. In fact, statistics say that the more preparation that's needed—driving, changing clothes, paying, signing up, etc.—the more likely you are to miss sessions and to drop out completely. Perhaps that's why the average membership at some health clubs lasts only three months. All you really need to do is to be sure your clothing is comfortable, your shoes are appropriate, and any equipment you use is safe.

On the other hand, be sure you set the stage for feeling good. You want the experience to enhance your self-esteem, mental well-being, and disposition. Some people need to look great, while others simply have to put themselves in a good frame of mind. It helps to make up positive mental images—perhaps about past successes. Take a couple of minutes to visualize the good feelings you'll have as you get into the workout. Remember the good feelings from the past, picture your hard stomach, firm buttocks, clear mind, and trim waistline. All of these thoughts will set you up for a better experience.

Warm-Up. Warming up may be boring, but it's essential. Take a few minutes to gently stretch and warm the entire body. A good warm-up will have you starting to break a sweat but not breathing too hard just yet. Give special attention to any sore spots and protect any injuries you may have. Some activities require 5 minutes to warm up, while others require 20. You'll have to decide by asking questions and observing other health-conscious people who are good at the activity.

Training Phase. The training phase is also called the aerobic section. Don't confuse this with aerobics classes; aerobic means literally "with air," or related to getting oxygen into the lungs and blood stream, as opposed to anaerobic, which implies short bursts of activity that do little for the heart and lungs. Aerobic types of exercise involve the large muscle groups in repetitious kinds of activities, such as bicycling, fast walking, jogging, swimming, aerobics classes, and rowing.

Cool-Down. You need to understand the reasons for winding down your workout slowly, because without a gradual cool-down you may get dizzy, faint, or overtax your heart. Here's why. After the preparation, warm-up, and workout, your body has been geared up to a high level of functioning. While exercising aerobically, your heart is being assisted by the large muscle groups of your body. These muscles act as secondary pumps helping to get waste-filled blood back through the venous system and to the lungs for the fresh oxygen exchange. Veins have one-way valves so that when the blood is pumped against gravity it won't drain back between heart beats or muscle contractions. Each heartbeat and muscle contraction help supply the body's increased oxygen needs. If you stop suddenly, much of the pumping action has been lost, the blood pools in the lower extremities, the brain does not get the oxygen it needs, and the heart is overworked. Keep moving. The ideal is to gradually slow the activity down until your breathing is close to normal.

Acknowledgment. Acknowledging yourself can take the form of a reward or a mental pat on the back. You have just completed something that will assist your body and your career. You should be proud. No doubt you're busy, but this reward time is what ties the ribbon on your program. It builds the mental connections you'll need in down times. Each time you think of exercising, you'll remember the good feelings and pleasant experiences you get from your program.

TAKING RESPONSIBILITY FOR SAFETY

One final point: Safety gets management attention at your workplace, and it should also be a primary consideration in your fitness program. Many joggers and cyclists are killed each year. You have a responsibility to do everything you can to make exercising safe. As a participant or observer, or even when you're driving your car, taking precautions and being alert can save years of healthy living from being wasted in an instant.

I'm occasionally criticised for using scare tactics in my classes and articles. I'm convinced that it's worth scaring a few people to get their attention with vital information that can save their lives.

LEARN TO LIKE IT

How do you learn to like something? Let's say you haven't found an activity that fits the criteria and makes you laugh. By heavily reinforcing an activity with positive statements, rewards, and pleasant images, you can actually learn to like something that starts out as unpleasant. Remember to surround it with good things and don't get hurt too often.

During high school and college, I was fanatical about participating in gymnastics programs. For most of us on the men's team, the pommel horse—one of the men's events—could be a deadly enemy because it had so much potential for injuring knees, ankles, wrists, forearms, and one's pride. Nobody particularly enjoyed working on "the pig," as it was affectionately known. To learn to like it, we set personal goals, organized team contests, and finally resorted to moving it closer to where the female gymnasts worked out. These tactics worked so well that a couple of the guys even gave up other gymnastic events to devote themselves entirely to the pommel horse!

You may have attitudes "for" or "against" something related to exercise. Attitudes have roots in our childhood discipline, culture, role models, and other memorable experiences, and if you indulge them, they can put limits on your accomplishments. If you find yourself expressing a strong belief mixed with a bit of emotional attachment or disgust, you have probably stumbled across a personal attitude rather than a universally recognized truth. Thank goodness attitudes can be changed! If you genuinely want to alter your attitude about exercise so that you can add this new power into your Careerstyle, then you need to gather facts, solicit feedback, and pinpoint how exercise fits in with your master plan for professional balance.

FOR FURTHER READING

Agress, Clarence. *Exercise Your Way to a Longer and Healthier Life.* New York: Grosset & Dunlap, 1978.

Cooper, Kenneth, M.D. *The Aerobics Program for Total Well-Being.* New York: M. Evans, 1982.

Cooper, Robert. *Health and Fitness Excellence: The Scientific Action Plan.* Boston: Houghton Mifflin, 1984.

Jacobs, Don. *Getting Your Executives Fit.* Mountain View, CA: Anderson World, 1981.

Kuntzlman, Charles, and the Editors of Consumer Guide. *Rating the Exercises.* New York: William Morrow, 1978.

Rayman, Rebecca. *The Body in Brief: Essentials for Health Care.* El Paso, TX: Skidmore-Roth, 1989.

Sorensen, Jacki. *Aerobics Lifestyle Book.* New York: Poseidon Press, 1983.

POINTS TO REMEMBER/THINGS TO DO

1. Always get medical advice.
2. Exercise with *consistency.*
3. Exercise with *moderation.*
4. Exercise with *variety.*
5. Include skating, dancing, walking, and other active outings in your social life.
6. Your heart rate (pulse) is a direct measure of doing too little or too much.
7. Pick exercises that are fun.
8. Learn to enjoy activities that combine social, exercise, and even career goals.

MY FITNESS INVENTORY

As a first step in your physical fitness assessment, answer these questions:

> 1 = Never, none, no way
> 2 = Sometimes, maybe, almost
> 3 = Always, definitely, yes

STRESS MANAGEMENT

A. I consciously improve my eating habits when under stress.   1   2   3
B. A little exercise does more for me than an alcoholic drink.   1   2   3
C. When I'm mentally tired I exercise anyway.   1   2   3

FLEXIBILITY

A. With my legs straight, I can easily touch my toes.   1   2   3
B. I can sit cross-legged on the floor for five minutes.   1   2   3
C. My back doesn't arch when both arms reach straight up   1   2   3
    in the air.

EXERCISE

A. I exercise aerobically three or more times every week   1   2   3
    (jog, bike, swim, fast walking).
B. My entire body is conditioned by the exercise I do.   1   2   3
C. I do different types of exercises regularly.   1   2   3

EATING HABITS/NUTRITION

A. I usually eat three balanced meals every day.   1   2   3
B. To lose weight I cut down on portions rather than   1   2   3
    skip meals.
C. I've usually eaten my last meal 4–5 hours before going   1   2   3
    to bed.

LIFESTYLE CONTROL

A. When my fitness lifestyle needs changing, I just do it.   1   2   3
B. I set fitness/health goals and objectives.   1   2   3
C. I'm satisfied with my physical fitness.   1   2   3

MEDICAL

A. Every two years my body is completely examined by   1   2   3
    an M.D.
B. I go for months without getting sick.   1   2   3
C. I am free of the risk factors of heart disease (high blood   1   2   3
    pressure, obesity, smoking, family history of heart disease).

SUBSTANCE USE/ABUSE
A. I go for weeks at a time without smoking.   1 2 3
B. My weekly limit of alcoholic beverages is under   1 2 3
   seven (per week).
C. The *only* pills I take are vitamins/supplements. 1 2 3

ON THE ROAD
A. When driving or as a passenger, I use a seat belt.   1 2 3
B. I always adjust the seat for lower back comfort.   1 2 3
C. On long trips, I walk and stretch every couple of hours. 1 2 3

CARDIOVASCULAR SYSTEM
A. After hard exercise I catch my breath within 60 seconds.   1 2 3
B. I take my pulse while resting and exercising.   1 2 3
C. My pulse returns to normal within minutes after exercising. 1 2 3

WORK/EMPLOYMENT
A. I take care of my health no matter how work is going. 1 2 3
B. I stand, stretch, and walk several times a day.   1 2 3
C. When traveling or working odd hours, I maintain an   1 2 3
   exercise program.

PERSONAL LIFE
A. I have enough energy for an active social life.   1 2 3
B. When looking in the mirror (full length), I'm pleased 1 2 3
   with what I see.
C. My vitality comes across to my spouse/partner.   1 2 3

TOTAL =

SCORING:

ADD 1 POINT FOR COMPLETING THE PFQ* SURVEY

    90 –100 = Outstanding
    70 – 89 = Good
    50 – 69 = Fair (some areas need work)
    34 – 49 = Poor (focus on low scores and retake in four weeks)

*(PFQ = Physical Fitness Quotient)

3

NUTRITION AND WEIGHT CONTROL

Wait! Before you skip this chapter let me say a few things about nutrition that just might persuade you to read on. First of all, remember that good nutrition, like exercise, should be one of the building blocks of your Careerstyle. You can't deny that a car runs better and longer when the right type of gas is used. And because you're an ambitious person, you want a high-performance body. Good nutrition, along with reasonable exercise and basic business skills, is part of the foundation of an achiever's lifestyle.

So how do you know what's good for you and what's not? Advertisers are constantly citing research to support useless products, but common sense tells us that we're hearing a biased view. How can you get all the facts and eat responsibly without risking being labeled a nutrition fanatic?

If you believed all the ads, you would eat nuts before dawn, drink gallons of milk for breakfast, munch on McNuggets for lunch, snack on Snickers in the afternoon, and slip slices of steak from the grill at dinnertime. Your evenings would be spent smashing beer cans or dancing with a mutt named Spuds.

KEEP READING

Guilt may have been another reason you thought about just skimming through this chapter. Let's face it, all of us eat the wrong things from time to time. This plug for good nutrition is meant to teach you three things:

1. First, you do need to know and review the basics of nutrition. We learned all the nutrition rules as youngsters, but may have forgotten them or just pushed them aside.

2. Second, it's perfectly okay to mess up and eat anything you want once in awhile. This book is about balance, and the trend of your diet is more important than rigid adherence to rules. It's more important that you feel good about yourself and keep your self-esteem up to par.

3. Finally, this chapter, along with the entire book, is designed to give you skills and attitudes that will allow you to naturally incorporate good habits into your life. When this happens, you will automatically select the best things for your lifestyle without giving it a second thought.

NUTRITION AND ACHIEVEMENT

If you can get a handle on what you eat and how much you weigh, you're probably a good candidate for running a successful business or department within an organization. Many of the requirements for running your personal life apply to running your business or your career, obtaining an advanced academic degree, or operating a professional practice or clinic.

What you eat and the amount of fat on your body will help or hurt your career aspirations. Whenever one part of life is out of balance, the rest is in jeopardy. It may take months or years, but when the pressure is on, a poorly fed and unfit body will let you down.

I enjoy long-distance bicycling, and regularly do organized 100-mile trips (also known as century rides). On one ride I made the mistake of eating poorly the night before, and skipping breakfast that morning. To top it off, the organizers only had cookies and lemonade at the morning rest stop. Even though I was in good bicycling condition, my body taught me how long and miserable a ride could be without eating well.

26

GETTING THE EDGE

Professional auto racing is a good example of the payoff for paying meticulous attention to every detail. Each driver's support team rigorously practices and refines every procedure in the hope that a tiny improvement may knock a split second off the time clock. Aerodynamics are refined, the tires have just the right amount of air, and the engine is built to harness all the horsepower it can. Good nutrition should be thought of as a similar advantage that will help you win the race.

FOOD ATTITUDES

A classic TV sitcom scene has the mama trying to get the son or daughter to eat the right foods while the irritated child rushes to get out of the house to get important things done. Well, mama has the right idea. The food we eat determines what our bodies have to work with. It also determines how well our minds can focus on the urgent issues of running a career, business, or department. In Western societies, we're surrounded with socially acceptable eating habits that—if you indulge in them—can slowly kill you or restrict your ability to achieve your goals. Culture is a primary influence on what we eat; nutritional patterns vary between cultures, and this shows up in differences in death and sickness rates.

If nutritional habits had an immediate effect on the amount of money we make in business, America would be bankrupt. The Standard American Diet (SAD) is filled with excess fat, cholesterol, sugar, salt, alcohol, tobacco, refined foods, and chemical additives. All of these items have been shown to be associated with the diseases from which we suffer as a nation. Recent announcements by the Surgeon General stamp the brand of approval on what we've been saying for years: Lifestyle habits directly affect the depth, width, breadth, and length of your life.

The significance of a good or bad diet sometimes gets obscured by other negative lifestyle habits, or the effects don't show up for a while because of the resilience of our bodies. If negative results were to occur right away, more of us would rush to adopt healthy diets to support our goals. However, we're so unaware of the consequences of the nutritional choices we make that we manage to ignore the troops of dieticians, educators, and health consultants that beg, plead, and cajole us to eat right.

THE BASICS

The first nutritional expert whose training you may have managed to ignore was probably your sixth-grade teacher, who taught you the basic food groups. If you do nothing but practice what your grade-school teachers taught you, you'll be in pretty good shape!

The basics include eating three meals a day, choosing a balanced diet from the four food groups, and keeping the right proportions of fats, carbohydrates, and proteins. The four food groups are: grains and cereals, meats and proteins, fruits and vegetables, and the dairy group. During any day you need to eat something from all of the groups. The American Dietetics Association recommends a diet consisting of 50% carbohydrates, 20% protein, and 30% fat. We should cultivate a taste for less salt, because even without adding it from a shaker, most processed foods already have large amounts of sodium even if we cannot taste it.

WEIGHT CONTROL

Americans spend billions of dollars each year to find the formula for losing weight. There are as many weight-loss programs and diet fads as there are flavors of ice cream. Before you spend your money and your time, let's look at the basics of weight maintenance.

One pound of fat contains 3500 calories. Basic weight loss boils down to burning more calories than you are consuming. This is called negative caloric balance. Experts (not fad diet promoters) agree that the ideal method is to lose a maximum of one to two pounds of fat per week. If you're not exercising and you lose more than that, you're probably burning muscle. If you *are* exercising and you lose more than that, chances are you're losing water.

The goal is not to lose a lot of pounds; the goal is control. A deficit of 500 calories a day will burn off one pound of fat a week. This approach allows you to make healthy Careerstyle changes that will last. A side benefit is that the change will be gradual and fewer people will notice. Some people don't like co-workers and friends to know they're trying to lose weight because they're afraid they won't succeed.

Psychological, sociological, and even anthropological studies have uncovered a pattern well worth noting and applying to lifestyle changes: The most permanent changes in individuals, groups, or cultures seem to take place over an extended period of time. It takes considerable time to positively alter the psychological make-up of an individual. At the cultural level, decades may pass before the positive effects of well-planned social programs take effect. The principle seems to be that good change is slow, consistent, and gradual.

CONTROL

A few words about control. It's important to make a distinction between weight loss and weight control. Control means you have a mastery or basic understanding of some process or principle. A monkey can lose weight, but it takes a thinking human being to control weight.

The enlightened person does not jump for joy when the bathroom scale shows that they've dropped several pounds, because he or she knows that it's a predictable result of something they're doing. They completely understand the process of caloric balance and even become concerned when they lose too many pounds in a short period of time. Let's talk some more about the infamous bathroom scale.

FAT VS. HEALTHY TISSUE

When you hop out of the shower and dry yourself well to get those "heavy" drops of water off before you weigh yourself, you should know that scale weight is deceiving. Bodyfat percentages give a better picture of weight maintenance than does the bathroom scale. A sensible program of diet and exercise will not change scale weight for as long as four to six weeks. It will, however, make a significant effect in bodyfat percentages. The battle relates to fat vs. healthy tissue. When you stand on the scale and it looks as if you haven't lost an ounce, you may have actually lost seven pounds of fat and gained seven pounds of healthy tissue! At the initial stages of your weight-control program, measure inches rather than pounds.

If you reduce calories to lose weight but don't exercise at the same time, you'll definitely lose weight. However, inactivity will also cause you to lose muscle. A ten-pound loss may actually be three pounds of fat and seven pounds of healthy muscle. As you lose that healthy tissue, your health will take a nose-dive, and this will affect your level of accomplishment. It's also an inefficient way to manage your weight, because muscle tissue consumes calories, even when you're resting. The message is to keep in shape. The shortcuts to proper weight control lead to loss of energy, frequent colds, and a lousy disposition.

Muscle is dense—a little weighs a lot. If you combine diet and exercise, your body exchanges fat for vital muscle tissue, bone, and blood. This is the safest and most successful method of weight maintenance. Research shows that rapid weight loss makes a person more prone to subsequent rapid weight gain. Unfortunately, you will not read that in many of today's diet books.

A TYPICAL CYCLE

Pete and Ralph are good friends with a lot in common. Both are college graduates, they are both happily married, and both enjoy good food. Their wives think they should lose a few pounds to regain the look of the college days. Pete decides to crash diet, and Ralph takes the slow approach that includes three weekly workouts. Within four weeks, Pete has lost a whopping 23 pounds with his fast diet, while poor Ralph has only a six-pound loss to show for all his time sweating.

Four months later, Pete has gained back the 23 pounds *plus* three extra pounds, while Ralph is down 20 pounds, looks great, and eats what he wants.

QUICK FIXES

Short-term achievers will do almost anything if it means a quick and easy way to lose weight. The amount of money spent on powders, pills, and additives has made more than one health product promoter smile all the way to the bank. It's my opinion that people who are susceptible to these kinds of swindles are also probably marginal performers in many other areas of their lives.

Professional marketers, recruiters, and interviewers are trained to spot the "quick fix" mentality. They know that this shortcut attitude is never isolated to one part of a person's life. If a prospect shows quick-fix tendencies in the services they buy, the marketer rarely expects a long-term relationship. When a recruiter spots the graduating professional's shortcut decisions, the session is over, and when the interviewer uncovers an area in which the candidate demonstrates little patience, they get the form letter ready to send.

If you don't have the rigor to learn about good nutrition and weight control, you have missed the first step. If you actually learn the principles but fail to apply them in your life, you might as well not have learned them in the first place.

There is a story about the "richest man in Babylon." Wealth seekers traveled miles and miles to ask him about his secret for amassing great wealth. His old schoolmates came to see him one day and asked him why, since they had all grown up together, the gods had favored and blessed him more than they? His reply was that the gods had not favored him more than any of them, and that if they had not acquired large fortunes, it was their own doing. They had either not learned the laws of building wealth or they had not applied them. And so it goes with weight control and many of the stepping stones to making it in life.

EXPERT ADVICE

Before seeking sensible advice, many people try bizarre combinations of fruit, powder, rice, and every other diet mentioned on the six o'clock news. Salespeople know that when a prospect wants the product badly, the sale will be easy. If the prospect is desperate or embarrassed and the product claims to solve the problem, the sale is a snap. Most dieters succumb to many sales pitches and diet fantasies before finally listening to the expert dieticians. The funny thing is that this advice is not only the safest and most effective—it's also the least expensive in the long run!

When people whose bodies and diets are out of control finally seek expert help, many dieticians begin by putting them on a regimen of three meals a day. To some dieters, this is as frightening as jumping the Grand Canyon on a motorcycle. Their way of losing weight has been filled with harmful shortcuts, one of which is usually skipping meals.

Hospitals are now offering expanded weight loss programs. If you need professional medical attention, we recommend that you enroll in one of these programs. If your problems are mild, a good understanding of weight loss, weight control, and body composition can save you a lot of time and money. This knowledge and application can get you on your way to higher and higher achievement. Here's more on what's happening in the "battle of the bulge."

MIND AND BODY

Mind and body are inseparable. What you eat affects you physically and mentally. Mood swings, depressions, and emotional shakeups can be fatal to the professional's career. You cannot afford not to take good care of this important foundation to your Careerstyle.

If you want long-term results, you have to be persistent in sticking with a sensible nutrition and exercise program until it begins to work. If you hang on a bit longer, you will begin to internalize the activities that lead to good nutritional and weight control habits. Variety in diet and exercise will keep you interested. There is no need to be afraid to try new foods or combinations of the old standbys.

Moderation in all things is a time-tested maxim. If you lapse and down a whole six-pack, there's no need to give yourself a black mark. Living moderately means that it is rare that you do this, but you do cut yourself some latitude to enjoy life.

NUTRITION AND BUSINESS

Business people are always eating. Your calendar may routinely include breakfast meetings, business lunches, and those dinner meetings that never end. In spite of the fact that a lot of business is done over loaded plates, not many very successful people are fat. The problem is—how many are malnourished? Few of us have learned to take care of our nutritional needs while in the environment of our jobs.

The basic food groups are available in any restaurant in any city; from Fresno to Frankfurt, you can find healthy food. You don't need to limit yourself to the menu selections—special requests are always acceptable in respectable establishments. You can ask for salad dressing on the side, leaner cuts, trimmed meat, and less salt, sugar, and cholesterol; restaurants are accustomed to these reasonable requests made by people who are going places and know that a healthy body will help get them there. Chefs throughout the world are beginning to offer healthier choices for those who prefer to live longer and achieve more.

Fast food has a bad reputation. Most of it deserves it, but there is an assortment of healthy food at most fast food outlets. Salad bars are turning up everywhere, and turkey, chicken, and juices provide some good combinations for excellent quick meals. You should first learn what fits into the basic food groups, watch the fat content, and then pick things that you like.

You can even bring great food from home. Leftovers warmed in the microwave make for some exquisite lunchtime items.

BIASED RESEARCH

A word of caution as you try to find solid information on food: the research quoted by advertisers is an unreliable basis for designing your diet. There are many reputable research organizations doing top-quality work, but their studies have trouble competing for public attention with the heavily funded research commissioned by product sponsors. The result is that you get half-truths and incomplete results in TV and magazine advertisements. If a tobacco company advertises research findings, you can bet they're in favor of smoking or they would not have released the results. Listen carefully to the research cited in the ads. "Most doctors agree" means that as few as 51 out of 100 agree. The other 49 may have valid reasons for not agreeing.

A person in a white lab coat may not really be a learned scientist but the same actor that does dog food commercials. Gray hair, rich furnishings, and a roaring fire in the background don't make the message any more mature or accurate. Caveat emptor—let the buyer beware—is not an empty phrase in the area of nutrition and weight control.

For most people, body appearance is closely linked to self-esteem. Advertisers are masters at exploiting this link. People with low self-esteem tend to be a more vulnerable to advertising that suggests that a product will make them younger, sexier, and thinner. For a look at a healthier self-image, see Chapter 10.

EATING UNDER STRESS

When the pressure hits and the stress levels soar off the charts, achievers know what to do. This is the time to use extra discipline about eating well, because the body, mind, and career need it more than ever. Think of the people you know who, when the pressure hits, lose their appetite, eat junk, and sacrifice their healthy routines; their competitive edge disappears.

Chapter 9 and the appendix will give you specific skills for dealing with stress in your life. When tough times roll in, successful professionals like yourself, knowledgeable in Careerstyle, roll out a combination of professional skills, personal discipline, and strategic balance.

FOR FURTHER READING

Bailey, Covert. *Fit or Fat: A New Way to Health and Fitness Through Nutrition and Aerobic Exercise.* Boston: Houghton Mifflin, 1978.

Bayrd, Ned, and Chris Quilter. *Food for Champions: How to Eat to Win.* Boston: Houghton-Mifflin, 1982.

Kuntzlman, Charles, and the Editors of Consumer Guide. *Rating the Exercises.* New York: William Morrow, 1978.

Natow, Annette, and Jo-Ann Heslin. *Nutrition for the Prime of Your Life.* New York: McGraw-Hill, 1983.

Reader's Digest Editors. *Eat Better, Live Better: A Commonsense Guide to Nutrition and Good Health.* New York: Reader's Digest Association, 1982.

POINTS TO REMEMBER/THNGS TO DO

1. Eat three meals a day.
2. Eat smaller meals (but eat something!).
3. Good eating starts with good *shopping*.
4. One pound equals 3500 calories.
5. If you don't burn the calories, they've got to go somewhere.
6. Healthy bodies burn more calories even while *sleeping!*
7. Make your goals public and visible.
8. It's okay to splurge once in awhile.
9. Food affects your career success.

MY EATING INVENTORY

SHOPPING: Start by buying groceries from all four food groups.

GRAINS/CEREALS   MEATS/BEANS/PROTEINS

_____   _____

_____   _____

_____   _____

DAIRY PRODUCTS   FRUITS/VEGETABLES

_____   _____

_____   _____

_____   _____

REGULAR MEALS: Check the food groups you include at each meal.

	BREAKFAST	LUNCH	DINNER
Grains/Cereals	☐	☐	☐
Meats/Beans/Proteins	☐	☐	☐
Dairy Products	☐	☐	☐
Fruits/Vegetables	☐	☐	☐

SNACKING: List your most common snacks.

1. _____   2. _____

3. _____   4. _____

5. _____   6. _____

SKIPPED MEALS: Which meal do you skip most often?

☐ Breakfast
☐ Lunch
☐ Dinner

4

TEN ACHIEVEMENT FACTORS

Careerstyle is based on strategy. Your strategy for professional balance and power requires a broad perspective and discipline. You can achieve a balanced, successful life by applying a combination of business career principles and personal development fundamentals, and by staying with this approach over the long haul rather than just as a quick experiment.

In this chapter, you will be given access to the ten Achievement Factors that allow you to combine business, health, and behavioral skills in a way that locks good habits into your lifestyle. It has been said that it takes 21 days to make a habit. If that's the case, you can create miracles by spending three weeks focusing on making a habit of putting the Achievement Factors to work in your daily life.

PRESIDENTS AND PREMIERS

The Achievement Factors were purposely developed to show how successful doers get things done and still lead healthy and balanced lives. My research took me to biographies of historical personalities like Lincoln, Roosevelt, and Alexander the Great. These guys weren't perfect, but they left legacies of useful strategies for achievement. I included current presidents, celebrities, and premiers along with national business leaders—all in an effort to find what makes them tick and keep ticking.

I came up with ten factors for achievement, which I then tested in large and small companies, government agencies, men's groups, women's groups, health clubs, trade shows, and even on family members. This chapter puts some well-researched information at your fingertips. Putting it into practice will take some work on your part, but it's definitely worth the effort.

39

There are no bargains at the success counter. We have to first learn the factors that make for high achievement and then we have to apply what we have learned until it pays off and becomes a habit. Of those reading this chapter, five to seven percent of you will read these ten factors, study them, reread them, and apply them. The other 93 to 95 percent will read them over and say, "Interesting, these are great," but unfortunately that's where it will stop within a few minutes, days, or weeks. I challenge you to be in the smaller percentage group.

I suggest that you list all ten Achievement Factors on a sheet and make a column for each day of the week. (You can copy the Inventory at the end of this chapter.) Each day, as you practice each factor, make a check mark next to it on the sheet. Keep the sheet publicly posted and reward yourself when you hit all ten in a two- to three-day period. Later you'll want to be more demanding before accepting the rewards. Let's take a look at these ten principles.

#1: ACTIVITY TAILORING

Tailor your Careerstyle strategy according to your strengths and weaknesses. You are the only one who can decide what you are truly good at and what areas may be weak points. Baseball, football, and basketball coaches place players in positions that will exploit their full potential. You are the coach of your life. Your task is to match your capabilities to projects that have the best potential payback.

Time management research provides a good example. Effective Time Managers (ETMs) have been studied extensively. One of the consistent findings is that ETMs are good at scheduling difficult activities during their high-strength times of day and their boring or low-urgency tasks during their low-energy times of day. The essence of activity tailoring is to know yourself well enough to give yourself the right jobs at the right times.

Good managers are required to know their workers so well that they can assign tasks according to strengths, weaknesses, preferences, and strategic directions of the organization. The logical extension of this process is to manage one's personal duties and activities so that they match up with good and bad points. This may mean that mail should be put aside until the drowsy 3:00 hour and the marketing plans outlined first thing in the morning if that is your most alert and inspired time of the day. As your skills change or the requirements of day-to-day living take on new twists and challenges, activity tailoring will keep you on track and effective.

#2: BEHAVIORAL TRAINING EFFECT

Play a note or two, write at least one line, read one page, or do one push-up. This is a take-off from the exercise physiology research that suggests that in order to become fit, you need to work out three to five times a week, with your heart reaching its training zone for at least 15 minutes each time. The Behavioral Training Effect is a a similar habit-building and maintenance technique: Whenever you decide to add something to your Careerstyle strategy, you must do part of it *every* day. In order to build the habit, your brain must experience a part of the activity each and every day. Even a small effort done daily helps to form your habits.

If you have decided that exercising is part of your plan, then do some activity every day. Now that you know the basics of good physical fitness, you won't be fooled into overdoing it, but you can turn it into a rock-solid lifetime habit by doing some part of it every day. It may be walking to the post office, pedaling five times on the exercise bike, or swinging a racquet five or six times before heading off to that important appointment. This approach may do nothing for your actual fitness, but it does wonders for your habit building. The behavioral part means that you do something. The more you do, the more it will be internalized.

If you have decided that becoming a better salesperson is essential to your long-term plan, the Behavioral Training Effect factor says that *every* day you must read, study, or practice some aspect of becoming a better salesperson. Some days it may be just a token activity related to good selling, but the point is that you did something.

It works in finance, too. Many Americans are out of control financially. Use this Achievement Factor in a two-part program. First, start saving $1 a day; and second, reduce expenses by $1 a day. This builds the habit of savings and control. You'll raise the amount automatically.

This brings up the subject of excuses. We can all think of someone who is a master at coming up with good, sincere, and believable excuses. Even with their good excuses, what do you think of these people? Are they achieving at an optimal level? How well are they respected behind the scenes?

For the highest achievers, no excuse is acceptable. If it truly could not be done, no excuse is necessary. There's some truth to the saying, "Never make excuses—your friends don't need them and your enemies won't believe them anyway." In many cases, there really isn't enough time to do a complete job or do a full workout. This Achievement Factor provides a method by which you can take a small step toward any goal, and it also takes advantage of the principle that motivation is higher in activities that are begun, as opposed to those not yet started. Do part of your goal *every* day.

#3: The 3-4-5 RULE

A continuous fuel supply is the key to Achievement Factor #3. The 3 is for three meals per day, 4 is for the four food groups, and 5 is for five glasses of water per day. It's risky to boil down a mass of good nutritional information into a simple 3-4-5 rule. Fundamental nutritional information is a must. It is worth taking the time to study food groups, proteins, carbohydrates, fats, metabolism, and so on. However, most of us need something a bit catchy that's easily remembered and reasonable to practice.

Three meals a day is the dietician's first priority for restructuring a client's diet. For example, breakfast: after an 8- to 12-hour fast each night, the body needs fuel. For those who do not yet eat breakfast, the thought can be repulsive. Like the first initiation to cigarettes, beer, oysters (and even kissing!), some things start out repulsive and seem to

42

get more attractive with continued exposure. It's really not that difficult to start out with a very small breakfast (fruit, toast, yogurt) just to build the habit (remember the Behavioral Training Effect?).

You've probably heard the saying, "Eat like a king for breakfast, a prince for lunch, and a pauper for dinner." The idea is to spread food intake over three meals with the bulk of calorie intake earlier in the day. This provides constant fuel for the body throughout the day without the spikes and valleys caused by varying blood sugar levels.

A widely varied diet including foods of different colors is a good way to help you get some of each food group into your body each day. You may not get all four at breakfast, but sometime during the day you need servings of breads and cereals, fruits and vegetables, dairy products, and meats and proteins. When in doubt, eat a wide variety of foods and see that there is an assortment of colors on your plate. It starts with your shopping list, so be sure to put things from all four groups in your shopping cart.

Who can drink eight glasses of water a day? Congratulations if you can! As a kid I tried, and was almost thought to have bladder problems because of how often I went to the restroom. Five glasses of water separate from meals is reasonable and do-able. Ten to fifteen sips at a drinking fountain should equal one glass for the average sipper. Avoid drinking water for about a half hour before meals or an hour afterward—when you drink liquids close to mealtime, they interfere with the digestive process. Before a meal, the water you drink will pass through rather quickly. After you eat, it takes 60 to 90 minutes for your stomach to complete the first stages of digestion. Water you drink during this time dilutes the digestive juices. Other liquids are usually fine with meals, but note that coffee, tea, and juices do not count as part of the five glasses required each day.

#4: GLOOM AND GLORY PREVISUALS

To gear up for high achievement in business or fitness, we need to practice or "dry run" the process of magnificent achievement and unfortunate failure. Gloom and Glory Previsualization means going to the movie theater of the mind and watching full-length mental motion pictures of you in action. See, feel, hear, taste, and smell the best and the worst that can happen. One thing that successful high-level executives have in common is that they usually go through best- and worst-case scenarios before they decide what course of action to take.

In creating this imagery, you have many options as far as what to do first, how intense the imagery should be, and whether you should down-play the negative side. Each person should tailor this Achievement Factor to their temperament and needs.

Here are instructions for a "glory-gloom-glory" combination. First, select something that is important for you to do well in the next three weeks. Now imagine doing it without a flaw or hesitation. Run the projector in your mind so that it is real and you are there. Next, take the same situation and imagine several problems occurring while you are doing the task. Run the projector and notice that even though bad things are happening, you are handling them. You may feel some anxiety. If it gets too uncomfortable, back off and "watch" it from a distance. Finally, replay the flawless version so that your successful achievement is firmly embedded in your mind.

Gloom and Glory Previsualization takes a realistic approach to positive thinking. Your physical condition, preparation, and mental attitude will determine how well you do in most cases. Sometimes, however, you won't have much control, and the best body, preparation, and attitude will still lead to a fiasco. That is where the high achiever shines. The test is how well you recover, gather your self-esteem, and press on to make the corrections needed to tackle the world.

When the real-life downturn hits, someone who imagines the glory alone will curl up and hibernate until the world stops picking on them. Others who actively practice the full version of this Achievement Factor will bounce back with more vigor and determination. Each one of us makes a personal decision.

#5: ACTIVITY LEVERAGE

You spend your time calling the right people, making important personal appointments, and writing key letters. The trick is to leverage these activities so that inputs and resources are carefully managed to maximize results and outputs. Leverage does not mean frantically working harder to get more done. One step at a time will get you nowhere. Taking one step at a time keeps you with the pack.

Balanced achievers know that to stay balanced in many areas, they must get the most output for every activity. Activity Leverage means that for every detail you handle (phone calls, memos, letters, presentations, etc.), you must leverage it to get the highest yield possible. Better yet, this high yield must be in strategic areas that build on your overall plan. An investment that yields the same amount as the initial balance is a waste of time.

One example of leverage is the manager who makes a work announcement to a group of ten co-workers at lunch rather than talking to each one individually. Another example is that of writing one good letter to the right customer at the right time, rather than three different letters to the wrong customers at questionable times. Good leverage is like the marksman who, with one deliberate shot, nails the bullseye, rather than the amateur who sprays the target with buckshot.

Successful achievers tend to have activities working for them in a synergistic fashion. Everyday achievers do X amount of work and only get X amount of payback. They remain with the herd. High achievers do X amount of work and get an X-Y-Z payback, usually to the utter amazement of those around them. Activity Leverage means that every X of activity must be carefully placed, properly groomed, and eventually evaluated for effectiveness. Only then can you be sure you are getting full value for your time and effort. Anything less places you in the ranks of those who do not have the rigor to study and apply leverage (and that's not the category for *you*).

Leverage is usually one of the main factors accounting for the difference between average and high achievement in sports, fitness, business, and lifelong careers. You can dramatically increase your leverage by refocusing on your written goals and objectives. Of course, if you do not yet have written plans for your achievement, you have just found another way to increase your leverage!

#6: M2-LP

M2-LP stands for More Mistakes—Last Place. This is the Achievement Factor that most people have trouble believing. The high-achieving professional should make more mistakes and come in in last place more often. Our upbringing has been that it is noble to be in first place, eliminate mistakes, make the grade, and be on top. Little boys learn to make the most runs in baseball and football, while little girls are taught to score highest in gymnastics and piano competition. The side effect is a nagging fear of failure.

Psychologists use the abbreviation "FNE" to signify "fear of negative evaluation." We fear that we'll disappoint our parents, teachers, and coaches. As we grow older, the fear of failure focuses on dating, social approval, and job successes. Nowhere are we taught that a long-term strategy has a place for failure and coming in last place. The statistics on suicide point an accusing finger in the direction of high expectations without a place for failure.

M2-LP means that if we are not making our share of mistakes, we are in the wrong class. We haven't begun to stretch our resources and limits. A boys' soccer team that takes first place time after time is in the wrong league. An exception, of course, is when you get to the top of the top, but who has really reached the limit of achievement?

The idea of coming in in last place seems anti-American, anti-social, and backwards. But wait. What if our goal is to learn fundamental strategies for continued achievement and success? Going from last place to first is a major building block in the characters of great achievers. Many great U.S. presidents lost minor elections and even previous bids for the White House. Most great advertising campaigns have ghosts of previously failed efforts tucked away in some closet.

Every business with a successful product on the market can point out a couple on the junk heap. It takes failures to learn about success.

By progressively moving up to more difficult categories, you will occasionally come in in last place even though you gave it your best. The learning and growing experience will be great, not to mention the lessons in humility that are so valuable. Last place is only bad if you remain there or refuse to learn from the experience. The Japanese and Koreans are showing the world that they have studied well.

#7: SPACED DIVERSIONS

High achievers take more vacations. It may be a chicken and egg story, but the correlation is definite. Those who do great things leave room in their lives for diversions that make the routine seem less monotonous and boring. Vacations, sabbaticals, and long weekends seem to be the most common types of scheduled diversions. Additional routine breakers include lunch breaks, afternoon walks, stand and stretch breaks, and even deep breathing routines.

I call this a withdrawal type of spaced diversion. This means that you remove yourself from the activity in order to take a pause, refresh yourself, and recharge the batteries. The withdrawal diversion has a positive mental and physical advantage because it allows the conscious and subconscious a respite. When this happens, there is always a direct physical benefit that adds to the overall positive effect on one's eventual achievement potential.

Be prepared—most people report that during withdrawal spaced diversions, while the mind is unencumbered with the trivia of the usual routine, the creative juices begin to flow. Many business people, artists, and musicians claim to receive their greatest inspiration during these times.

A second type of spaced diversion is the substitution diversion, in which instead of stopping your work, you change something about the work. A writer can shift from working on a book to preparing a short article or doing research in another physical location. The gymnast can switch from the rings to the horizontal bar. The mental or physical output may be almost the same, but because different parts of the brain or body are being used, it feels like a rest, and it allows you to return to the original project without getting bogged down.

Most people find that the net result is that they get more done than if they had kept plugging away at the original project without the diversion. This second type is for those who feel guilty taking a real break or genuinely have so many other projects that substitution is required because other important work has to get done.

If you have outlined your Careerstyle strategy, you may have found that you need incredible amounts of time and energy to accomplish your goals. Spaced diversions allow you to schedule your life so that more gets done without draining your resources and your zest for life.

#8: 3-FOR-1 SALES

Hit all the 3-for-1 sales of life. It requires that you STOP, CLEAR your mind, and THINK. The average achiever thinks about getting two things done in one trip to the grocery store. The average professional gets two things done in one client visit. The exceptional achiever STOPS, CLEARS the mind, and THINKS about a third thing that can be accomplished with the same amount of time and effort.

A word of caution: this Achievement Factor is not suggesting that you do three things at once. That's a sure way to go crazy. The 3-for-1 sale means that you're doing an extra item without the extra trip or the extra effort.

The engineer who schedules a one-on-one meeting immediately after a group meeting is an average achiever. The one who meets with a small group before the meeting, has the notes typed during the meeting, and has the personal meeting after the group meeting is hitting the 3-for-1 sale of the afternoon. Three trips and three conference room reservations were turned into one.

It's a good idea to sandwich different parts of your lifestyle into the 3-for-1 concept. For instance, *walking* to a restaurant, *discussing business* with an associate, and *eating a healthy noon meal* is the essence of the 3-for-1 concept, and is one of the foundations of the Careerstyle strategy. You may want to review the Achievement Factor on leverage.

#9: EXPERT GOAL SCHEDULING

Successful professionals make their goals realistic, specific, and written. Realistic goals mean that with a running start (and a good breakfast), you've got a very good chance of making it. Stretch goals are more difficult and also have their place. As long as you've "stretched" your category (see M2-LP), you are already in a difficult league and now is the time to set realistic step-by-step goals that will keep you progressing and smiling. If you're staying in the easy league, you'd better start setting sky-high goals if you want to achieve anything remarkable. If you are in the proper category, relax—you're probably progressing well.

The trick is to keep your courage up and give yourself lots of mental pats on the back. Without them, you'll become bitter and discouraged. Realistic goals, like IBM's sales goals, are reached about 80% of the time, so if you're not always at 100%, you're nevertheless on the right track for success.

Goals need to be very specific in order to eliminate ambiguity. When you write down the results you plan to achieve, define how you will measure the outcome and specify the timeframe for accomplishment. Someone besides you should be able to read the goal, measure your progress, and determine whether it was completed within the timeframe.

Why hide your goals? If you really plan to achieve them, then post them in the most visible place you can find. This will remind you constantly of your intention, and it will also let anyone who comes along know what you're doing so that you get reminders from other people.

Most goals get filed . . . mistake #1. Most goals have no ongoing review . . . mistake #2. High achievers live their goals day in and day out. You don't file away your plans for how you're going to live on a daily basis. Your goals should be in your path and reviewed constantly.

Intel Corporation, one of the largest semiconductor firms in Silicon Valley, actively participates in the United Way fundraising campaign each year. During the campaign, most entrances to Intel buildings have an easel with a thermometer painted on a board. Progress toward the goal is graphically painted in red to signify what percentage of the goal has been reached. Everyone from production worker to top executive knows how well the company is doing every single day.

Make your goals realistic, in the right category, specific, and visible and be ready for opportunity to start knocking. You'll be prepared.

#10: INPUT INCUBATION

In business, as well as in health and personal development, it can be devastating to launch into an activity based on your first impression or experience. A first step in a proposed project is to communicate your thoughts, ideas, inclinations, and opinions to other people. You'll be surprised at how many people have thought or felt the same way. Input Incubation allows new inputs into your Careerstyle to settle a while. This Achievement Factor suggests that you take a second look at your initial inclinations.

In business many pride themselves on making fast decisions or barking out decisions made on the fly. Careful follow-up shows a poor batting average for those who shoot from the hip too often. The professional who uses silence and listens carefully can take new inputs and incubate them based on an overall strategy. This is the only way to be sure that your actions and decisions are leading you in the direction for which you have painstakingly created a strategy.

A good idea today will probably be a good idea tomorrow. There are exceptions, but not many. This should not be used as an excuse for procrastination. If a decision must be made and the risk involved in delay is great, make the decision. On the other hand, good professional decisions are well thought out. No need to take weeks or months, but some incubation time can work wonders. If time is tight, use the Spaced Diversions factor to speed up the "brewing" process.

In fitness, the best way to ruin a good program is to overdo it at the first session. I taught competitive gymnastics for years, and it got so that I could always predict when new students, eager to learn, would have trouble getting up and moving their bodies the next day. Input Incubation stresses that you test what you are putting your body through. See how it reacts to a certain level of intensity and go from there. The same applies to jogging, tennis, biking, racquetball, or swimming. Let the "input" incubate for a while and make your informed judgment about what intensity is right for you at that time.

ADDING POWER TO YOUR LIFE

I'm pleased when I hear people say that they heard about the Achievement Factors at some speech or presentation. Most people remember one or two that had a powerful impact on their life. I hope that you will read and review these factors several times so that their full potential can be realized in your Careerstyle. One or two will do wonders, but all ten used together will change your life, guaranteed!

FOR FURTHER READING

Garfield, Charles. *The New Heroes of American Business.* New York: William Morrow, 1986.

Giblin, Les. *How to Have Confidence and Power When Dealing with People.* Englewood Cliffs, NJ: Prentice-Hall, 1987.

Henderson, Carter. *Winners: The Successful Strategies Entrepreneurs Use to Build New Businesses.* New York: Holt Rinehart, 1985.

Musashi, Miyamoto. *A Book of Five Rings: The Classic Guide to Strategy.* Woodstock, NY: Overlook Press, 1974.

POINTS TO REMEMBER/THINGS TO DO

1. Review the Achievement Factors once a month.
2. Start with the easy ones to build habits.
3. Progress to the difficult ones gradually.
4. Keep track of how many factors you use.
5. Watch successful, balanced people to see how many Achievement Factors they naturally use.
6. Use notes and tickler files to remind you to use the Achievement Factors.
7. Reward yourself for consistently using the Factors.
8. If you fail or get depressed, see M2-LP.

MY ACHIEVEMENT FACTOR INVENTORY

Practice using the Achievement Factors for a week. Each day, check off those you use.

	MON	TUE	WED	THU	FRI	SAT	SUN

Achievement Factor #1:
ACTIVITY TAILORING ☐ ☐ ☐ ☐ ☐ ☐ ☐

Achievement Factor #2:
BEHAVIORAL TRAINING EFFECT ☐ ☐ ☐ ☐ ☐ ☐ ☐

Achievement Factor #3:
3-4-5 NUTRITIONAL RULE ☐ ☐ ☐ ☐ ☐ ☐ ☐

Achievement Factor #4:
GLOOM AND GLORY IMAGERY ☐ ☐ ☐ ☐ ☐ ☐ ☐

Achievement Factor #5:
ACTIVITY LEVERAGE ☐ ☐ ☐ ☐ ☐ ☐ ☐

Achievement Factor #6:
MORE MISTAKES/LAST PLACE ☐ ☐ ☐ ☐ ☐ ☐ ☐

Achievement Factor #7:
SPACED DIVERSIONS ☐ ☐ ☐ ☐ ☐ ☐ ☐

Achievement Factor #8:
3-FOR-1 SALES ☐ ☐ ☐ ☐ ☐ ☐ ☐

Achievement Factor #9:
EXPERT GOAL SCHEDULING ☐ ☐ ☐ ☐ ☐ ☐ ☐

Achievement Factor #10:
INPUT INCUBATION ☐ ☐ ☐ ☐ ☐ ☐ ☐

5

WOMEN: CLIMBING, GRASPING, AND GASPING

"If by strength is meant moral power, then woman is immeasurably man's superior.... If nonviolence is the law of our being, the future is with women." Mohandas K. Gandhi

There have been more changes in the role of women in the latter half of the 20th century than in the past five hundred years. Women are now in a position to make their own major life decisions. They no longer feel that their maternal responsibilities oblige them to sacrifice their youth, career, health, sanity, and self-respect.

When it comes to male-female protocol, the tide has turned even more than in the family setting. From the early 1950s all the way into the 1990s, feminism has grown into a full-blown revolution. Women will no longer be treated as helpless objects in need of constant attention and correction.

This chapter is addressed to today's professional woman, and is also good reading for the man who wants to understand the special stresses that affect the women they work and live with.

MALE REACTIONS

Men have been astounded by the things women have lately demonstrated that they can and will do. The male reaction to these changes has been rather strange; they treat these changes in women like they would the prospect of a truck coming directly at them late at night on the wrong side of the road, and they may immediately put up barriers. For many women, this is a signal to ruthlessly crush opposition. The cycle is then justified—the next step for these men is to put up bigger and better barriers! Or to carry on with the metaphor, they want to drive bigger trucks, or even tanks, in order to smash the women coming at them at full speed.

Other men join the parade and agree that they've been dirty rats and they won't do it again. Most women consider this group nonthreatening, which may be a misreading of the situation. These yes-men are often afraid to voice their true fears and apprehensions. They won't show any signs of opposition or lack of support. They've been won over too easily.

These men remind me of my graduate school days, when I did research on problem solving with middle managers. I was thrilled when three managers immediately agreed to be part of my thesis research. The other five gave me a tough time before agreeing. The early three assured me that they would do all that I needed, while the other five said they would try, but if pressure situations arose at work, they would not continue. My department chairman warned me to be careful of the ones who said yes to everything too easily. Sure enough, the tough sales were my best participants, while I ended up babysitting and holding the hands of the three easy catches.

Another group consists of men who are willing to reveal honest reactions to women's changing roles and voice those reactions as best they can. These are not the easy catches, and it is this group of men that offers women the best chance to make constructive changes in attitudes. Extreme reactions, whether positive or negative, eliminate healthy dialogue. The saying, "A man convinced against his will...is of the same opinion still!" does seem to hold water. These guys put up a good fight because they're being honest. But when they're finally won over, it's for real.

BIG CHANGES FOR WOMEN

A new area of initiative for women is the exercise and fitness field. The aerobics movement has shaped, toned, and invigorated those who participate regularly and consistently. It is perfectly normal for the woman who is an "exercise enthusiast" to get up early or stay out late in order to include a good workout in her busy day. On the other side of the coin, many other women have learned to drink and smoke just like men.

Women are entering midmanagement and executive-level positions at an increasing rate, and there is an associated trend to delay marriage in order to establish a professional base before beginning family life.

MARRYING LATER

The median age for first marriages among women is 23. This all-time high has taken more of a jump recently than the same statistic for men. It seems that both sexes are waiting longer, but women have been increasing their delay in marriage more than men.

Recent demographic studies have revealed surprising statistics on marriage probabilities that should give women more reason to build balance into their lives. You've heard the predictions that women with a college education who are still single at the age of 25 have only a 50% chance of marrying. This goes down to 20% for those who reach 30 and to about 5% for those over 35 who haven't yet married.

True, these statistics include gay women and women who choose not to marry or who do not think highly of the selection of available men. If you are a woman who wants a family life, your best bet is to include this goal in your overall plan for achievement. These statistics may apply to the average achieving woman, or to those who are focused only on their careers, but I believe that the balanced professional woman can build these goals into her lifestyle and daily activities and show that these figures are wrong for any healthy, well-rounded woman who knows the basics of achievement.

This chapter focuses on the juggling act that women often feel obliged to keep up when they seriously pursue a career, and how in too many cases their Careerstyle is mishandled. I do not intend to downplay in any way the major hurdles and barriers that women have already overcome, but the fact remains that most women have not applied their professional decision-making skills to their entire lives.

A MAN'S TERRITORY?

Until recently, it has been a firmly held tradition that the domain of business is a man's territory. Both men and women are beginning to deal with the changes that a woman's new role has made in family and interpersonal life, but the same degree of progress in the boardroom will take twice the effort.

Impressive gains have been made at the managerial level, with women now holding over 30% of management positions, but this does not mean an easy glide into top-level positions. Of course, many women are starting their own firms or progressing quickly in areas not dominated by men. Why will it take so long to enter high positions, regardless of the field? Traditional attitudes in the boardroom is one explanation. Another is money.

ROOM AT THE TOP?

Top executives earn enormous salaries, and boards of directors expect top performance in return for the salary investment. To break into these ranks, a woman must have more than one or two bright spots on her resume. It is only in the last decade or so that significant numbers of women have been getting the broad experience and opportunities that qualify them to even be candidates for high-level executive positions.

A final barrier is that women do have babies. There are several equal employment and affirmative action guidelines meant to keep employers from discriminating against women on the basis of potential or actual maternal responsibilities. Many enlightened couples do share childcare. However, except in unusual cases it is doubtful that large numbers of men will ever take an equal share of the responsibility for providing or arranging care for babies, youngsters, and teens. At the risk of being called unprintable names, I'll speculate that it is also very unlikely that women will do more combat time or heavy construction work than men.

LIBERATION OR BONDAGE

Professional women had an easy time in the first stages of real liberation. These professionals were usually assertive (in a good sense), intelligent, verbally fluent, and quite capable in their field. A lot of progress was made in a short period of time by some very sharp women.

Now the hard part. When it comes to running a professional career or a business, the professional woman will fail miserably in the long run unless she recognizes her own unique qualifications for success rather than mistakenly mimicking the neurotic lifestyle of men who are short-term achievers. The norm that many women have tried to imitate has led to physical neglect of their bodies, substance abuse, poor nutrition, poor mental health, and exaggerated expectations—in other words, following male models will lead women to the same place it has led men for centuries.

The statistics on female progress in the business and professional world are impressive. Equally impressive is the speed at which the negative side effects have attacked the minds and bodies of the professional women who had noble aspirations but followed the wrong example. I'll never forget overhearing a female manager telling a friend that since she now travels with male co-workers she has to "learn how to do more drinking."

IMPRESSIVE ACCOMPLISHMENTS

Twenty-five percent of all medical degrees are awarded to women. This is double the number granted ten years ago. Thirty percent of all law degrees are earned by women. More than 50 percent of all college and university students are now women.

The workforce recently passed a dramatic milestone when women passed up men as the majority of workers. From 1980 to 1985 the number of men in the United States workforce went from 49.8 million to 51.9 million, while the number of women jumped from 44.5 to 52.9 million. Back in 1940, women accounted for only 25.8 percent of the American workforce.

The Conference Board estimates that between now and 1995, women will account for two-thirds of the growth in the labor force. The second income provided by working wives is a major contributing factor to the trend of families moving up to middle and upper income brackets.

Women possess the intelligence and toughness it takes to excel, and they have shown amazing tenacity and ingenuity in breaking new ground for themselves. What about the cost to these hard-working women?

THE DOWN SIDE

Unfortunately there is a bit of trouble in Camelot. Newspapers and research journals are full of evidence of alarming side effects of women's quest for fast equality and quick achievement.

Several credible sources report that women are drinking more beer, driving sportier cars, and defending themselves more willingly in fist fights. We have long heard about the type A male who overworks, is given to shouting, and, in general, over-paces his life. This hard-driving guy gets a lot done, but also has more heart attacks. Now we have research on type-A women, who are exhibiting the same behavior as the type-A man, with the same results.

Women have now gained equality in cancer deaths. It is estimated that 38,600 women will die annually from lung cancer, which now surpasses breast cancer (by about 200 deaths) as the leading cancer killer of American women.

Ulcers used to be almost a symbol of anxiety among professional men. Advertising executives in 1950s movies are prone to clutching their stomachs when they hear bad news about an account, then fishing in their desk drawer for a handful of stomach tablets. Back in 1955, for every 20 males with ulcers there was only one woman, but in the workaholic 1980s, for every two males with ulcers, there is one female sufferer. Researchers at the peptic ulcer clinic at UCLA say that this negative trend is primarily due to the increase in the number of women who smoke. Smoking results in a reduction in bicarbonate (acid neutralizer), which lays the groundwork for a gastric or duodenal ulcer.

If you smoke, equality is already here: the longevity figures that show women outliving men by seven to ten years don't apply. The life expectancy for smokers is exactly the same for both women and men.

Alcoholism is a risk in any group trying to move quickly to achieve the finer things of life. The middle-aged man has been cast as the typical alcoholic, struggling to make it big in the face of insurmountable obstacles. More and more women have recently been diagnosed as having the same alcohol problems. Today, nearly half of the alcoholics in the country are women. The abuse of alcohol has increased three times as fast among women as among men. Recent research shows that women who drink more than moderately appear to have increased cancer risks.

FEMALE ACHIEVERS

Women who expect to break into new territory require a firm foundation of good health, clear thinking, and strategic business planning. There are no shortcuts and very few *appropriate* role models.

Networking has been going on for as long as there has been organized human activity—long before it became a catchword and topic for seminars. Ambitious people know how to tap all available resources, and many female networking groups have sprung up to make up for the headstart men have in business connections. This is fantastic as a first step; however, as soon as possible, the high achiever should mingle with groups that represent the real world. Business strategy dictates that one learns, lives, and breathes as much about her particular market and customer base as possible. Empathizing over breakfast is okay if it is followed by getting down to business before lunch.

If you are a woman who is serious about incorporating the concept of Careerstyle into your long-term strategy, you should know that three attitudes will determine how well you succeed: your willingness to pursue personal development and fitness, how you handle your anger, and how realistic your expectations are.

I'll deal with physical fitness first. Aside from helping you achieve a thousand goals, it can also be your best defense in case of physical assault.

HEALTHY WOMEN = POOR TARGETS FOR ASSAULT

Women are easier targets and generally more vulnerable to sexual assault than men. The attitude of confidence that comes with a superbly fit body is bound to show. That may be enough of a deterrent. If not, the fact that you are fit gives you the option of escaping or fighting back if you feel that would minimize your chances of injury. Recent government studies show that women who resist assault have fewer injuries and suffer a lower level of emotional trauma.

The same confidence works for you professionally—a physically confident woman is more likely to stand up for herself and to be treated with respect by her associates. An assault can be physical, verbal, or mental. Mental assaults, whether real or imagined, can be especially damaging to your confidence in your career and your capabilities.

Many women have felt the subtle pressure of a funny look, rolling eyes, being left out of meetings, or even being publicly patronized or ridiculed for their ideas. Any of these assaults at work can leave you confused and angry. Your health and balance just might get you through it without killing someone or using obscene language.

ANGRY WOMEN FALL SHORT

When it comes to rage, many working women are addicts. There is strong evidence that most high-achieving career women make great sacrifices to succeed at the earliest stage possible. When obstacles pop up, they sacrifice their personal lives. If their goals are still not achieved in spite of what they've given up, they may become bitter.

Here's the rub. Like racial minorities, professional women feel they've paid their dues. They have made the sacrifices, earned the degrees, done the traveling, and handled all the other nuisances they felt would earn the right to success, but success rarely happens on time.

The worst-hit are unmarried women in their 40s. The anger shows through all attempts to mask it. The catch-22 is that their careers may have been negatively affected by their anger, with the result that the personal sacrifices are guaranteed not to create success for them.

Much anger is justified, but a woman's reaction to the anger is what's important. I have worked for organizations on the East Coast and in Florida where women held most of the management positions in stable industries. In Silicon Valley in California, I've also worked with women in companies that were less stable or were in highly volatile markets. The women in the West seemed to have higher expectations, higher salaries, more stress, and more frustration with their careers.

Some of these women react by assessing themselves and their situation. They decide what they can do to cope with what they can't change and they fix what they can change. They don't harbor loads of resentment.

On the other hand, other women keep dwelling on the unfairness of their company or industry. You may have seen cases where this anger creates hostility, cynicism, and a very negative attitude. Their environment may not get better, but the women who cope well will create a better situation for themselves.

A WOMAN'S ASPIRATIONS

According to the Journal of Applied Social Psychology, high expectations usually result in higher payoffs. The one exception, according to the study, was when women made extremely high or low demands. The sky-high expectations tended to backfire.

In other words, women were less likely to succeed if they deviated too much from the norm. A good guess is that this results from the uncertainty associated with the shift that is taking place in women's roles, and that women will have more flexibility as their professional roles begin to settle.

Too many women are imitating the life-threatening patterns of men. Some men who are in high positions now are destined to failure in the long run because they didn't put balance in their lives. Women need to model on the truly successful achievers who strategize a firm foundation of health, fitness, career planning, and business acumen to reach long-term and lasting successes.

WHAT CAN YOU DO?

It's a good idea to find and study people who have already made it. Find someone who has been successful in your chosen field— someone who has kept her head on straight. You may find that she has gone through some confusing times too.

Another piece of advice is to be patient in those areas that are frustrating you. It's hard to be patient. It may seem like a cop-out or a lack of self-confidence that is keeping you from getting what you deserve. Hold on! Many of the men and women who have accomplished great things had to wait much longer than you have already waited.

Attend to the important and urgent things that must be attacked without delay—go after them with a vengeance! Do what you need to do now, and then wait patiently.

YOUR THOUGHTS ON FEMINISM

Feminism will be a touchy subject for a long time. Give yourself some peace of mind and clarify your personal views on this movement. Men and women will come closer together on the issues if each takes the time to think through their personal views and to listen to alternative viewpoints. As a woman, you are obligated to develop your personal view on your own movement just as if you were a member of any racial or religious group.

It's okay for personal views to differ from the majority. That's how most movements get started in the first place. Teenage girls, housewives, and career women are changing their attitudes on feminism. Many are refusing to hold past leaders up as current role models. This means that new thinking is taking place. You can let the pendulum swing back to a previous stage, or you can push the message forward with more effective methods.

CREATE YOUR SUPPORT SYSTEM

Women are fantastic at supporting and comforting one another, and often everyone around them as well. This has a positive effect on stress, anger, and even life expectancy. Female systems of support start to unravel as a woman begins to travel across the professional tightrope. Some think they should be strong at this level, and that begging for support and comfort is too soft and unprofessional.

Many men have been taught that it is a sign of weakness to ask for help, but a closer look at masculine systems shows that support *is* usually available for the smart professional. Just as atheletes have coaches, so do up-and-coming business people have mentors and buddies from whom they get feedback. Women can do as well or even better if they admit that they need this solace.

Typically, women feel stress in their professions, but this is probably no different from men. You will find it much easier to create a balanced Careerstyle if you let others know when you need help. Create your own support system in all the parts of your life. Cultivate people who are good "coaches." Ask for detailed feedback on your performance, and pay attention to what you're told.

There's not a single Olympic athlete who progresses to that level by themselves. Entrepreneurs may start companies alone, but the ones that grow and evolve do it with teams. The good and great leaders of the world make progress by using knowledgeable and loyal support systems.

NO TURNING BACK NOW

Women have come a long way, carving out huge new territories in all areas. A woman has more choices than at any time in history. Some women will continue to mimic the life-threatening behavior of their male predecessors, but a select few will systematically order their lives with the big picture in mind. These are the ones who will be on top in whatever field they choose.

FOR FURTHER READING

Brothers, Joyce. *The Successful Woman: How You Can Have a Career, a Husband, and a Family and Not Feel Guilty About It.* New York: Simon & Schuster, 1988.

de Beauvoir, Simone. *The Second Sex: The Classic Manifesto of the Liberated Woman.* New York: Vintage Books, 1974.

Dowling, Colette. *Perfect Women: Hidden Fears of Inadequacy and the Drive to Perform.* New York: Summit Books, 1988.

Mason, Mary Ann. *The Equality Trap.* New York: Simon & Schuster, 1988.

Phelps, Stanley, and Nancy Austin. *The Assertive Woman: A New Look,* 2nd ed. San Luis Obispo, CA: Impact Publishers, 1988.

Shaevitz, Marjorie Hansen. *The Superwoman Syndrome.* New York: Warner Books, 1984.

Witkin-Lanoil, Georgia. *The Female Stress Syndrome: How to Recognize and Live with It.* New York: Berkley Publishing Group, 1985.

POINTS TO REMEMBER/THINGS TO DO

1. The principles of *balance* apply to both women and men.
2. Excesses that harm men will also harm women.
3. There are excellent female role models in almost every profession.
4. Successful women tend to have *exercise* and *nutritional* goals.
5. Balance and consistency accomplish more than anger and resentment.
6. Identify two to three high-priority "battles" and fight them with a passion.
7. Never let men or other women do or say things that lower your self-esteem.
8. Review and use the Achievement Factors.

9. Try to find two to three new ideas or opinions from your male friends or colleagues.
10. Associate with balanced men and women.

MY GRASPING OR GASPING INVENTORY

	DISSATISFIED.......SATISFIED				
	VERY	SOME-WHAT	JUST-OKAY	SOME-WHAT	VERY
1. MY PRESENT CAREER	1	2	3	4	5
2. MY FAMILY SITUATION	1	2	3	4	5
3. MY ROMANTIC RELATIONSHIPS	1	2	3	4	5
4. MY FUTURE CAREER PROSPECTS	1	2	3	4	5
5. MY HEALTH AND FITNESS	1	2	3	4	5
6. MY EATING HABITS	1	2	3	4	5
7. MY DRINKING (Alcohol) HABITS	1	2	3	4	5
8. MY SMOKING HABITS (If you don't smoke, circle 5)	1	2	3	4	5
9. MY ACCOMPLISHMENTS	1	2	3	4	5
10. MY SUPPORT SYSTEM	1	2	3	4	5

TOTAL SCORE _____

---

40 to 50:
You are professionally balanced—keep *achieving!*

30 to 39:
You're doing fine but target 1 to 2 weak areas to improve.

10 to 29:
Watch out! You will begin to *gasp* without a good foundation.

6

MEN AND THE "LITTLE-BIG BOY SYNDROME"

There was a time when the American male essentially ruled the world. In international, national, and family affairs the American male had first, only, and final say. As world leader, the United States, run primarily by males, ranked as one of the greatest and most powerful forces of all time. The influence of the U.S. male in international affairs was unquestioned. This great country had natural resources, industrial capacity, and technological innovation, and with our American creative chutzpah we set the country decades ahead in commercial, academic, and military fields. Men were proud to be American males. The world looked to the men in America as leaders.

All this has changed. Women, international politics, and poor strategy have forced us to take a second look at man's role. Men have paid their dues in time, effort, and sacrifice, but no longer exclusively run the country or its major organizations. Although men continue to hold the larger share of management jobs, their share has declined over the last several years from 82% to 70%. Women now hold a full 30% of managerial jobs, and it didn't take long to jump from only 18%.

Time was when the old-boy network took care of things. Competition among men was fine, but let an outsider such as someone from a minority, a foreigner, or a female attempt to break in, and the full cohesive force of the male establishment would mobilize in subtle but effective ways. Right or wrong, this pattern was effective long enough to become ingrained in many male minds as both positive and acceptable.

MEN AND THEIR FAMILIES

The family unit has taken some near-fatal blows in the last couple of decades. Divorce has risen dramatically, and the incidence of child abuse, alcoholism, and drug addiction is up. In many families, the parents have one addiction, while their kids have another. Teenage pregnancies, abortions, and social diseases have also had a shaking effect on the family.

The male role has shifted from being the supreme authority and sole breadwinner; women now provide a significant share of the income. In some cases men have abdicated most family decision making. Many men feel they have simply lost control of their families.

In this chapter, we'll show that many of these changes are healthy adjustments. The balance we've been talking about applies to men at home, at work, and in anything they do.

The new family role for a man might be to take his daughter to soccer practice on his way home from work, and make dinner while his wife is pumping iron at the gym (where she bought her own membership).

STARTING THE "LITTLE-BIG BOY SYNDROME"

The Little-Big Boy Syndrome explains many of the emotions, behaviors, and frustrations of both men and women today. It is the consequence of little boys being told to act like big boys long before they had those skills in their repertoire. If by chance the little boy felt hurt, scared, and overwhelmed—no matter, he was to keep quiet, act like a big boy.

Not all men have been subjected to this kind of upbringing, but the majority were. Men still have trouble admitting it or discussing it, but many can trace current behavior patterns and stubborn opinions back to the Little-Big Boy Syndrome. It is a system that yanks little boys from the sandbox and squeezes them into narrow, masculine molds.

"Act like a big boy" is heard over and over by millions of young boys across the country. They hear it from mothers and fathers, uncles and aunts. Candy, movies, and small change are used to bribe little boys to stop crying, and being called a sissy is cause for a duel in the sandbox. The syndrome is evident at even younger ages where male tots trade in their fuzzy bears for the Joe athlete models or the war blasters eagerly given by adults. The little big boys are being molded to reject anything that shows weakness. They are learning not to cry and never to let a girl be better at anything.

MEN HAVE FEWER CHOICES

One result of this early learning is that men have fewer choices when it comes to emotional, social, and cultural changes. Society has done a marvelous job in passing on the "acceptable" culture to each new crop of male toddlers. Men are supposed to be strong, firm, and above all else, "right."

Little boys want to express themselves in whatever way feels best. Some want to cry, others want to talk, while still others want to run away. Anything is okay as long as it does not go against the role of the big boy they will soon become. Even if the young boy's parents avoid this syndrome, the roles in cartoons, movies, and commercials teach boys not to be weak. From bubble gum wrappers to comic books, little boys are being molded to be macho men.

Some men develop macho bodies, others acquire macho possessions, while still others have deep-seated macho attitudes. You can read the signs in clothes, cars, jobs, and attitudes. All of these make balanced achievement a nasty chore when male and female roles keep changing.

WIMPS AND SISSIES!

The natural reaction of an animal when attacked is to fight or flee. In earlier times, human beings responded to danger in much the same way. We either stood up and fought back or we ran for cover as fast as we could. We're still doing the same thing now, except that danger presents itself in subtle, new psychological and emotional forms—threats may be social, financial, or sexual. Fighting back no longer means clubbing the attacker to death. Running away is more than dashing for the nearest cave or clump of bushes.

The fight or flight decision had functional value. When the attacker was twice your size, it was nice to have a choice. Men do not have that choice. Of course no one forces them to stand up to every contemporary attack, but our culture strongly punishes men who flee. For example, politicians lose elections when they appear weak and wimpish. Executives lose their jobs when they give too much in a negotiation. Baseball managers who don't act tough and win get fired. The guy who doesn't compete usually won't get the girl. These are a few examples where a man's role dictates toughness, competitiveness, and a "take no prisoners" attitude. It's a model that's not only stupid, but unworkable as well.

A man's choice in a fight or flight decision strikes at the essence of his masculinity. He must perform well or step down in status. If he fights, he is called a no-nonsense man or an entrepreneur. If he runs away, he is labeled a wimp or a sissy.

To create true balance in his life, a man's decisions should be based on long-term goals, not on reflexes left over from his "little-big boy" training. Men cannot afford to continue pursuing goals from a warped perspective.

FIGHTING BACK AND PERFORMING

It's not surprising that grown men feel responsible whenever anything goes wrong. They've been bred to be in charge and to act decisively. As leaders of nations, industries, and families, men have had first-hand or role model experience in being the one to get the job done.

They'll automatically fight anything that looks like failure, embarrassment, or weakness. Most men have a mental flag that says, "Uh, oh—watch out! Here is something that may make me fail, look stupid or appear weak...attack!" This mental flag has been on extra duty now that women are sharing responsibility at work and at home.

After being told not to cry, not to give up, and never to fail, the next part of their training was to ask a girl out, pick up the tab, acquire a car, never look weak, and be great at sports.

As adults, men must bring home a good paycheck regardless of economic times, perform well in bed, and trot off to war with a stiff upper lip. A man's career, portfolio, and social standing are expected to be exemplary. Any deviation means that this guy somehow missed part of his upbringing and is not a good provider or role model.

The most serious conflict arises out of the limited ways a man has available for attacking when threatened: on one hand men must stand tall and have a backbone, but on the other hand, they are supposed to be flexible, sensitive, and caring. This confusion of responsibilities isn't reasonable or realistic. Something is bound to break. Instead of losing status, most men will choose to fight back. This has some devastating mental and physical consequences.

It is possible to fight back in constructive and positive ways, and we'll deal with this later in this chapter. In the meantime, let's look at how some men have chosen to cope with the Little-Big Boy Syndrome and the results of some of those choices.

ONLY THE MEN DIE YOUNG

Men tend to deal with this problem in some dangerous ways—criminality is one extreme response, while other men internalize the stress and no one knows until they drop dead. The stress of living out the Little-Big Boy Syndrome is one reason men live on the average for about 71 years while the female lifespan (except for women who smoke) is a full seven years longer. The little-big boy who shuts up and keeps it all inside turns into the man who does not show feelings and is labeled insensitive.

Expressing feelings seems to give women an edge in reducing pent-up stress, emotions, and despair. Studies show that after the loss of a spouse, women consistently recover better than men, largely because it is acceptable for them to confide in others. All the evidence continues to show that men who have not learned to "let it out" are paving the way for long-term problems. The average male body can hold repressed anger and anxiety just so long until eventually the Little-Big Boy Syndrome claims another tight-lipped victim.

A special feature of a popular morning weather forecast is the reading of one or two birthday letters about people who have reached the 100-year mark. Many more women than men are announced in this segment. There may be a gender-related genetic factor that explains why men die younger than women, but most of the difference is in lifestyle. Women whose lifestyles resemble those of men die earlier. Life expectancy rates are highest in Hawaii and lowest in Washington, D.C. Even though men are always on the short end, this regional difference means that lifestyle and environment have an effect on how long we live.

LIFE'S STEADY LEFT JAB

Hemingway's *The Sun Also Rises* immortalizes the running of the bulls or "encierro" in Pamplona, Spain. People (mostly men) race through the streets in a drunken and adrenalin-crazed stupor. Inches behind and sometimes on top of them run a pack of snorting, angry bulls. An American was recently gored and hospitalized. He later snuck out of the hospital to finish "running the bulls." He said he needed the excitement in his life at least once a year so he could really let go and get his blood pumping. He used the Henry David Thoreau quote that says, "The mass of men live lives of quiet desperation," to explain why so many, like him, need some kind of relief.

76

It is a shame he has to risk his rear end to let off a year's worth of steam. A better strategy for releasing steam is to let it out as it accumulates. That is what balanced achievement is all about. You cannot fight back by swinging wild punches. Some will connect, but most likely you'll be the one who gets "knocked out" with life's steady left jab.

Part of that "quiet desperation" comes from not knowing how to respond to the women's movement. Most men have been severely chastised, in public, for some *faux pas* or chauvinist remark. Few men have steered clear of some embarrassing slip-up. The problem is that often the poor guy had no idea his remark was so offensive. Most men would gladly make quick efforts to improve if approached in a humane and respectful way.

The U.S. Weather Bureau provided a small token when they began naming hurricanes with both men's and women's names. We now have hurricane Bob, Ignacio, Kevin, Danny, and Gilbert, as well as the traditional female names, for tropical storms. It sounds a bit like "by-the-book parity" where everything in the world must now be his/her, chairman/person, mankind/womankind. Men, like women, will not be fooled with token gestures that do nothing to hit at root problems like the Little-Big Boy Syndrome.

TEN MOST WANTED LIST

Men have usually been the perpetrators of crimes. Because of the Little-Big Boy Syndrome, men have more of a tendency to lash out in unacceptable ways than women. Anger, fear, and quiet desperation can't be bottled up indefinitely. Only in the areas of child abuse and alcoholism do we read about as many female abusers as male.

The FBI took a reporter's suggestion and published a list of the criminals-at-large they wanted most to capture, and they began circulating the Ten Most Wanted list. It wasn't until 1969 that the first woman, Ruth Eiseman-Scheir, broke into this male-only club. Since then there have been fewer than six women on the list.

77

Crime should know no gender. The problem is that the U.S. Dept. of Justice reports that 5.1% of the males born in the United States will serve time in an adult state prison. Men are imprisoned 14 times more frequently than women.

With these statistics, it would be easy to think that men are naturally inclined to violence. Is there a genetic difference that explains this tendency? I doubt it. It seems to be a failed part of the male socialization process.

The questions and answers are complex, but much is the result of men being forced into square boxes when they may have wanted to beat round drums.

IT'S NOT THE GENES

Justice Department statistics show that imprisonment rates for all categories of men and women have increased, but the highest rate of increase (43%) has been among white females. This tragic result is an outcome of women trying to copy male expectations and behavior patterns without first weeding out the ineffective and harmful portions (see Chapter 5).

For the first time, there are large numbers of women following in male footsteps, and when their new roles lead to some old problems like ulcers, lung cancer, stress, and unbalance, we can make an educated guess about which parts of men's traditional roles are harmful, and we can change some of the usual ways of doing business in order to stay healthy and balanced.

Men have not known what to change, but now there is a whole new group of players—women—who have entered the fast-track game.

Some of these women have added formerly male behaviors such as smoking, drinking, compulsive working, and physical inactivity to their lives. The visible effects are disease, stress, confusion, and failure. The writing is on the conference room wall.

78

TAMING THE SYNDROME

The Little-Big Boy Syndrome pushes little boys so hard that they end up fighting bulls, wars, women, and their own feelings. The method of choice in combatting the Little-Big Boy Syndrome focuses on balancing rather than fighting. When it comes to the women's movement, any attempt to counterattack can easily lead to excesses in the opposite direction. Men need to avoid needlessly antagonizing groups that have legitimate claims mixed in with excessive demands.

Some men ridicule the more outrageous feminist demands and discount the entire message. The logic of refuting the excessive demands may be correct, but the strategy is lousy. Groups tend to make excessive demands when some of the basics are missing. There really are some legitimate gripes.

The women's movement at home and at the office is no exception. Part of the message is a demand for change. Another portion, especially with male-female roles, is in consciousness-raising. Women want men to think about the issues. The balanced male will see this as a change rather than an attack. Men who felt attacked in the 1980s will be either beaten or balanced in the 1990s. There will be little room for them to pick a position in between. Men can start to tame the syndrome by understanding it.

In all fairness, men have been getting mixed messages. Charges of sexual harassment at work have been flying, yet we constantly see articles in women's magazines proposing detailed plans for snaring the man of their dreams. Men can't help noticing that these articles suggest in some detail what clothes, perfume, accessories, and even business terms women should use to help in their apparently all-consuming mission.

Men see ads for workshops that teach women how to nab a man. Several books talk about "man hunting" and selecting a job based on the "male quotient." This last one identifies the "male quotient" as the number of eligible men easily accessible to a woman in various positions.

79

Granted, men should be able to sort out illegal sexual harassment from genuine personal interest, but it does create confusion.

Most professionally balanced men take the issue very seriously. They have made personal and policy changes to be sure that women can perform their duties and advance fairly without sexual intimidation. The legal message seems to be "Hands off." The practical message appears to be "Read the signs."

Harassment goes both ways. I once did a consulting job for an organization in Florida that had a budget of more than $4 billion. I field-tested a publication that included a feature on sexual harassment, and was practically executed. The women in the company said that their organization is 75% female, and that *they* usually do the harassing, so I'd better go back to California and change all my examples of men hitting on women to more realistic cases of female supervisors going after men's buns. I dutifully rewrote the section. It turned out to be effective and rather fun to do.

We often hear that there are not enough men around. What women mean is that there are not enough heterosexual men at the status level they want. The message seems to be "Get out there, guy. They want you." Many of the sought-after men are out of sight because they're fed up with the hassles of the changing times and careers. A more balanced approach would be for a man to appropriately test the water without harassing and to explore his own background and feelings.

Our culture has programmed men and women to act in their roles. As the roles change there will be a clash between one's upbringing and current standards.

WHAT CAN MEN DO?

The key is balance. If the men of today are to continue to achieve their goals, they must refocus their strategy to include the basics of Career-style. Only by balancing professional needs with good personal development will they be able to withstand the new pressures and changes coming from every direction.

Some of you reading these lines are thinking, "I can handle it my way," or "It won't be as bad or last as long," or "I know what's best." Sure you do, but remember that a lifetime of conditioning has trained you to think that way even when another approach would be more successful. Read on and put the little-big boy thoughts aside.

A clear and balanced set of achievable goals is a must. They should be personal and they should be written down. The Achievement Factors in Chapter 4 should be mastered and tied to your goals. You may feel that your old methods got you this far and there is no need to change. Once-great nations, organizations, and families have had the same delusion since the beginning of time, and they have fallen when conditions changed.

Reversing some of the effects of the Little-Big Boy Syndrome is a slow process, but so is building a successful career. You may not see that fitness, good nutrition, and stress management are directly related to reaching your goals. However, the net effect will be a solid foundation for high achievement in all aspects of your life.

Instead of feeling alarmed at reports of the "decline of masculinity," take a look at the big picture. Right or wrong, the issues are on the table and must be resolved. Men will have to direct their professional careers and their health and fitness lifestyle toward the achievement of their personal goals, not as a response to conditioning about how men are supposed to be.

It's okay to cry, it's okay to fail, and it's not a sin to finish in second place. In the future, men will be judged less by their bank accounts and more as whole, balanced people. The Little-Big Boy Syndrome can be understood and even corrected by presenting young boys with better models and by giving grown men balanced options.

FOR FURTHER READING

Astrachan, Anthony. *How Men Feel: Their Responses to Women's Demands for Equality and Power.* New York: Doubleday, 1988.

Goldberg, Herb. *The Hazards of Being Male: Surviving the Myth of Masculine Privilege.* New York: Nash Publishing Co., 1976.

Halper, Jan. *Quiet Desperation: The Truth About Successful Men.* New York: Warner Books, 1988.

Klein, Edward, and Don Erickson, Editors. *About Men: Reflections on the Male Experience.* New York: Pocket Books, 1987.

Levinson, Daniel. *The Seasons of a Man's Life.* New York: Ballantine Books, 1978.

Trachtenberg, Peter. *The Casanova Complex: Compulsive Lovers and Their Women.* New York: Poseidon Press, 1988.

POINTS TO REMEMBER/THINGS TO DO

1. The principles of *balance* apply to both men and women.
2. Pick two to three things from your childhood that affect you today.
3. Discuss these past events with someone you trust.
4. Separate what you do for your goals from what you do because "you're a man."
5. Try to find two to three new ideas or opinions from your female friends or colleagues.
6. Do nothing that lowers your self-esteem or the self-esteem of others.
7. List four to five professional needs *and* four to five personal/ emotional needs.
8. Weigh your two lists against each other in terms of their importance, the degree of fulfillment they provide, and their contribution to your having balance in your life.

MY "LITTLE-BIG BOY" INVENTORY

TOYS I RECEIVED AS A BOY:
1.
2.
3.

SHOWS/CARTOONS I WATCHED AS A BOY:
1.
2.
3.

GAMES I PLAYED AS A BOY:
1.
2.
3.

MY CHILDHOOD HEROES AND ROLE MODELS:
1.
2.
3.

REASONS I WAS PRAISED/REWARDED AS A BOY:
1.
2.
3.

THINGS I WAS PUNISHED FOR AS A BOY:
1.
2.
3.

EMBARRASSING SITUATIONS FROM MY CHILDHOOD:
1.
2.
3.

WHAT I LEARNED AS A BOY THAT STILL AFFECTS ME AS A MAN:
1.
2.
3.

7

SEX AND PROFESSIONAL BALANCE

You will recall that Careerstyle links all parts of your life.
Sex is a part of your life's pattern, regardless of what your sexual
preferences are or what your upbringing and sexual experience
may have been. Your attitudes on sex have already molded major
portions of your personality, your aspirations, and even your daily
activities. For example, some of you have read all the previous
chapters, while others flipped directly to Chapter 7!

Sex is often used solely as an attention getter. I remember
attending a general meeting at a religious university. I have
forgotten all that the speaker said except for one single word.
He knew he was in a religious setting and he wanted to break the
ice. He did it by repeating the word "penis" rapidly fifteen times.
It had quite an effect on the audience. The goal of this chapter,
however, is not to shock or titillate you—it's to take a look at
sex in the context of our achievement.

We are all intensely interested in this semi-taboo area of our
lives. When we were kids, we weren't supposed to talk about it,
but "everyone" did. When we were teenagers, we weren't
supposed to do it, but "everyone" did, or so we thought. Now, as
adults, it's time to take control of our sexual well-being so that it
contributes to our success and happiness. Now is the time to
look at sex outside of textbooks, joke books, and medical
articles and see how it can add balance to our lives.

This chapter is no substitute for good medical information.
Medical information on sexual functioning, dysfunction,
and disease is critical as we approach the year 2000.

In fact, it's so important that it may determine whether or not we make it to the new century at all! Seek it out and use it.

Achievement is usually associated with a person's professional life. Unfortunately, some people allow themselves to accept a gap between professional goals and personal relationship goals. They aim high for professional marks, but leave their personal lives to chance. The purpose of this chapter is to discuss the way in which sexual intimacy relates to your progress in life, and to encourage you to take control of this most intimate area of your Careerstyle.

CHICKEN AND EGGS

Napoleon Hill, in his multi-volume series on *The Law of Success,* said that successful and high-achieving people are usually highly sexed. There are two implications behind Hill's statement: one is that achievement by itself is sexually attractive—that fulfilling and frequent sex is one of the rewards of accomplishment. The second possibility is that good sex may lead to high achievement—that sex is a stepping stone along the path of achievement. This chapter will explore both of these ideas and we'll take a look at how high-achieving men and women can fit pleasurable sex into their Careerstyle.

Most of us are still bashful about this most intimate part of our lives. We keep hearing that it's healthy and even fun. We know that it's okay to talk about it, but we still fear how our friends, relatives, or associates might react if they knew what we really think and do. Sex is a power-packed topic that still borders on being taboo.

VARIETY OF SEXUAL ENCOUNTERS

Let's start with an overview of the four types of sex the balanced achiever is likely to encounter at one time or another—sex with strangers, with acquaintances, with lovers, and with spouses. I'm not saying that we all will experience each of these sexual situations, but they will all be available in some form. The level of achievement that each of us will attain is influenced by how we handle these four types of sexual situations.

We're going to talk about heterosexual encounters, but the same principles apply to homosexual and bisexual experiences. The chapter ends with a discussion of some of the current trends in sexual relationships and their possible effects on balanced achievement.

SEX, MONEY, AND POWER

Sex itself is so powerful that even hints, implications, and gossip about the F-word can lose kingdoms, ruin presidential campaigns, and get you a guaranteed appearance on every talk show in the country.

Sex, along with money and power, are the semi-taboo topics of our age. Most men and women feel a little uncomfortable letting others know how much they want and need all three, because they so intimately involve our self-esteem. The result has been a rash of popular books, articles, and workshops that teach us to obtain sex, money, and power for ourselves. The high achiever learns early that having a lot of money or power attracts the other two—anyone with money will have power and available sex, and vice versa. That is one good reason for taking the time to put sex in perspective and make it fit properly into your life.

STRANGERS IN THE NIGHT

Sex with a stranger is the first form of sexual encounter we will discuss. This is the one-night stand so popular in the late Sixties and Seventies— a sexual encounter with a stranger that usually starts with small talk in a bar or night club, progresses to drinks or dancing, and ends up at either person's home, a motel, or even a car. This encounter seldom leads to one of the other three kinds of sexual relationship: one or both people may be embarrassed by the casualness of the experience, or afraid the other person is a regular at sexual encounters of this sort.

In the Eighties, changing lifestyles and values shifted the scene for casual sex away from bars and into singles groups, health clubs, and other ways of meeting people. Aside from personal value judgments, achievers take care to evaluate how this level of sexual encounter fits into their strategy for life.

Morality is not the issue. The question of balance is the key to this type of sex. Each individual achiever will decide if his or her unique pattern of success has room for sex with someone they just met, and the fear of deadly sexually transmitted diseases has become a potent factor in this decision. Some people manage to keep the one-night stands in their lives undercover, while in other circles, casual sex tends to be regarded as a badge of achievement by both men and women. Each individual must find his or her own way of either managing or eliminating casual sex.

SEX WITH ACQUAINTANCES

It was just a friend or co-worker and you ended up in a tempting situation that became intimate. This can be shocking, confusing, and scary. Most people claim they wish it had not happened. Others say that it has zero effect on the friendship or working relationship. Here is another sexual situation that most professionals will probably come up against. Many will actually have intercourse, while others will just flirt with the temptation.

This second area involves sex among longtime friends as well as casual acquaintances. As a result of close working, living, and playing conditions, it is quite common for two people to end up in an intimate situation without actually planning for it to happen. Whether or not it leads to sex depends on other commitments, moral values, attractiveness, alcohol, drugs, emotional state, and hundreds of other factors.

Sex among acquaintances can have an effect on the rest of your life, because unlike a sexual encounter with a stranger, you can't just call a cab and forget it ever happened. You still have to see the person, work with him or her—maybe even live with them. Here is another area where a person's security and self-esteem come into play. Sex with an acquaintance is neither right nor wrong in the context of creating a balanced Careerstyle. Those with solid self-esteem and confidence can handle the morning after, or the days after, and can communicate feelings of ecstasy, disgust, bliss, or shame in a way that sets the issue to rest or allows the relationship to develop. The balanced person knows that clamming up announces your shame and disrespect for yourself and the other person.

Your goal should be to respond in a mature and professional fashion. Both of you have lives to live and achievements to pursue. Whether or not you actually make love, the feelings are there, and these desires and temptations need to be resolved or they will sap your energy. Dealing openly shows that you are an adult, that you control how you act, and also allows you to consciously decide whether or not to pursue a relationship.

Love relationships at work are becoming more common for several reasons. It eliminates the risks involved in dating someone you know little about. There are more opportunities to learn all about a person that you work with daily. To use sales terminology, when you date people you work with, you have "qualified" prospects to choose from. You know a lot about their livelihood, their reliability, and even their friends. These factors may balance out the potential problems of becoming sexually involved with someone you work with.

SEX BETWEEN LOVERS

The difference between having sex and making love involves much more than sexual intercourse. Sleeping with a lover involves regularity and learning about your partner. Communication and intimacy begin to grow, and turn having sex into making love. This two-way sharing serves the achiever, and goes way beyond a simple release of tension. Releasing tension can be great fun, but if there is more to be gained from a good long-term sexual relationship, the high achiever will make room for it.

It is possible to treat a regular sexual relationship as if it were a series of one-nighters with the same person, or to have a courtship that develops quickly into marriage. Most relationships fall somewhere between these two extremes.

Your mental health and self-esteem are very much affected by how you handle ongoing sexual relationships. On the one hand, relationships take time and energy, and problems with a lover or spouse usually result in poor performance at work and the loss of a person's zest for life. On the other hand, single professionals who manage to build stability in their personal lives benefit in the areas of self-esteem, stress management, and general well-being.

AFTER THE WEDDING

Most of us were taught that we would grow up, fall in love, get married, and start having sex—in that order. This archetypical pattern is seldom followed anymore, and young adults feel less pressure to marry predictably and on schedule. However, most people feel drawn toward settling down and marrying that perfect person, and we also appreciate having the benefits of fitting comfortably into the accepted social order and letting the world know that we are "normal" human beings. Statistically, marriage seems to be on the rise again, but having a lifetime partner is no guarantee of a satisfying sex life.

Sex within marriage can have just as many problems as any of the other three types. Couples often fall into the trap of taking their sexual lives for granted, and gradually noticing that they're bored. The common response to a lackluster sex life at home is to dive into work or some other diversion. At this level of sexual encounter, a diversion is the least effective way of creating a full, satisfied personal life.

Most couples do not want to acknowledge that they have a sexual problem when it's merely a matter of boredom. Okay, maybe a better way to say it is that your routine sex life needs to turn into something a bit more stimulating. The effect of this boredom will go much further than the bedroom—your career will be affected. This means that if your sex life happens to be in the context of marriage, the quality of that lovemaking can have a big effect on your overall level of accomplishment and satisfaction.

Thousands of women responded to an invitation by Ann Landers to tell her whether they preferred cuddling and holding to the act of intercourse. The letters she received revealed the inexcusable laziness of many men, who failed to extend even the common courtesies of romance and lovemaking. Those who wrote in yearned to be held and treated with tenderness.

Chicago *Tribune* columnist Mike Royko responded with a survey of his own. He found that the large majority of men really do prefer sex with their wives to recreation such as bowling, fishing, golf, and so on. He did, however, receive some scathing accounts of wives who were guilty of the same types of uncaring laziness as in Landers' survey. The men said things like, "Foreplay consists of fifteen minutes of me begging." One wrote, "The greatest feeling in the world is going to the bowling alley...and knowing that your wife hates you because she knows you are in seventh heaven without her." Another letter from the same area of the country said, "I have a neighbor who prefers bowling to sex with his wife. So when he goes bowling, I have sex with his wife."

The married man or woman in search of a satisfying intimate life is no further ahead than someone who is unmarried, separated, or divorced. Each of us has goals to set and a strategy to map out, and everyone's sexual lives will be more or less satisfying at different times.

Married people probably feel less flexible when problems arise because of being attached to one partner. But a married person with a balanced strategy is able to respond effectively to sexual problems because he or she has developed a support system and the ability to communicate about sex as well as other intimate concerns. The well-prepared married partner stays fit and manages stress and other areas of personal development.

SEXUAL SUCCESS

Going back to Napoleon Hill's view that successful people are highly sexed, we find that whether or not he was right, success is closely tied in with sex. This may be a chicken and egg relationship, but there is no doubt that your management of these four categories of sexual intimacy can enhance or detract from the achievement of your present and future goals. Of course, after you have become famous (your definition of course), you may end up having better sex in any category you choose.

A word of caution on mixing categories. Sex in more than one category at a time or just in the first two may require an amount of time and effort that is disproportionate to the rewards. Your aim is to make choices that will help and not hinder your plan for achieving goals.

CURRENT TRENDS

Sexual values are changing rapidly as we near the close of this century. When we had Prohibition, the country went from wet to dry and then back, and sexual attitudes have also swung wildly. The late 1980s and 1990s are expected to mark a reversal from promiscuous sex back to traditional values. In the context of achievement (rather than sex therapy or a moralistic sermon), anything with the potential to detract from long-term satisfaction and fulfillment in life should be carefully managed.

It's interesting that the advertising industry uses sex appeal as its major draw. Money and power are not far behind in persuasive power. Sex is a primary human drive that motivates an amazing amount of human activity. Like air, food, and water, sex has extreme pulling power. All four of these can be beautifully managed or horribly squandered.

The Europeans have always had a flair for spicing up daily life with a little display of "tits and ass." Recently in French-speaking Belgium, billboards were used in a campaign to slow drivers down a bit. Drivers read either, "Driving fast is as stupid as making love fast," or "You do not seduce me when you go fast."

The Joy of Sex says that "Sex ought to be a wholly satisfying link between two affectionate people from which they emerge relaxed, rewarded, and ready for more." This "Gourmet Guide to Lovemaking" also says that "There are only two guidelines in good sex—don't do anything you don't really enjoy, and find out your partner's needs." So why does sex still get in the way of our using our full potential? Recent trends provide some insights into what's going on in our culture.

VIRGINITY AND DEFENSIVE SEX

What goes up must come down and what swings right also swings left. Researchers have noticed a marked conservative shift in recent sexual attitudes. Over 40% of college women said they were virgins in the late 1980s as opposed to 38% at the end of the 1970s.

There has been no such recent shift among men. Where men have changed is in the number of sex partners and the general amount of promiscuity. Men and women both say they have fewer sex partners, go for longer periods without sex, and at times masturbate more often. The reason seems to be the fear of herpes, AIDS, and other sexually transmitted diseases. We can also assume that the lawsuits for passing along sexual diseases have also played their part.

Defensive or "safe" sex has been used to describe a new scenario in the dating game. Because of the dramatic increase in social diseases, passion has been tempered with a heavy dose of paranoia. It is common practice to ask a date if he or she has any type of disease or condition that should be discussed before the relationship progresses. Defensive sex not only crops up before hopping into bed, but also later in the courtroom. Substantial amounts have been awarded after a partner has been infected with a disease the other partner knew was contagious. This can hamper anyone's achievement!

Winners in any activity, especially sports and business, tend to be proactive. They review information and act swiftly in their best long-term interest. Defensive sex is actually very proactive. It means taking acceptable precautions to ensure your own safety and that of any partners you may have. The creation of balance in your life requires at least this much. Taking control in this area includes the careful selection of partners, open communication about intimate matters, getting yourself educated on current medical knowledge, and having regular medical check-ups.

GUILT AND EROTOPHOBICS

Psychologists and sociologists who watch sexual trends have shifted their research away from liberal sexual attitudes back to the old-fashioned guilt research prevalent in times of strict social behavior. The study of erotophobia, or fear of sex, is getting renewed attention. Erotophobics are most often women; they tend to be intensely religious, come from strict backgrounds, and are less likely to get breast exams or visit a gynecologist.

An interesting report came out of Ciudad Juarez, Mexico where an 86-year-old woman went into the hospital with digestive problems. After taking X-rays, doctors found a 60-year-old full-term mummified fetus in her abdomen. She remembered feeling pregnant in her late twenties, but the child was never born and she did not miscarry.

ATTRACTIVENESS AND ACHIEVEMENT

Have you ever thought that only beautiful people drive BMWs? Or that great-looking men and women get promoted more often? Attractiveness plays a hefty role in both professional and personal arenas. Attractiveness between men and women has been studied in every conceivable context. Men are attracted to beautiful women, but luckily, beauty means different things to different men. A woman's beauty in the eyes of a college athlete will most likely differ from that of a 45-year-old accountant.

Women are initially attracted to handsome men, but actually focus more on a man's professional and social standing and—surprisingly enough—his humor. This alone can explain many couples that seem to be mismatched on the surface. Dale Carnegie wrote that if we want people to be attracted to us, we should dole out praise lavishly. He reasoned that this would be a competitive asset in goal attainment. Some men have obviously read that book a few times!

There is an interesting sociological concept called "equity theory," which says that we bargain and barter attractiveness for money, social standing, or prestige to make our personal balance sheets come out equal. My feeling is that attractiveness and achievement are closely intertwined.

Research pinpoints why both sexes feel there is a scarce supply of the opposite sex. Male attractiveness is based on social, economic, and political standing. Female attractiveness is usually based on physical beauty alone. These researchers say that the average female is more attractive than the average male. Most males are going after the attractive women, while the very attractive women are going after the few very successful males. Both have difficulty hitting the jackpot.

A final note on these interesting findings is that there is an almost universal tendency among women to want to marry up. The term is "hypergamy." It is said that women tune in to the traits in a man that signify high achievement, worldly success, and financial clout.

PROBLEMS FOR CAREER WOMEN

As we said in Chapter 5, career women are going through some difficult transitions. In pursuit of professional goals, many women put off personal relationships until later in their lives. Some are finding that their standards continue to rise with their level of affluence, but that the selection of available men that are acceptable to them dwindles.

Married career women report a different problem. The Masters and Johnson Institute reports that career-oriented women are turned off to sex more than any other female group. They are also more likely to suffer from vaginismus, an involuntary tightening of the vaginal muscles that makes it difficult to have intercourse. Researchers suspect that a major factor in this dysfunction is the career woman's reduced frequency of intercourse. It is interesting to note that although career women report many more sexual problems than women who hold traditional jobs or no jobs at all, their husbands report fewer cases of impotence than those married to unemployed wives.

SEXUAL STRATEGIES

The thought of including your sex life in your strategy of Careerstyle should make more sense now that we have looked at the career and personal implications of the four types of sexual encounters, and surveyed the current state of sexual relations in our culture. It's impossible to predict the future of relationships between the sexes in the twenty-first century. What we can say is that long and useful achievement benefits from what we do in the bedroom as well as what we do in the gym or the boardroom.

FOR FURTHER READING

Branden, Nathaniel. *Honoring the Self: The Psychology of Confidence and Self-Respect.* New York: Bantam Books, 1985.

Buscaglia, Leo. *Personhood: The Art of Being Fully Human.* New York: Fawcett Columbine, 1978.

Kent, Margaret, and Robert Feinschreiber. *Love at Work: Using Your Job to Find a Mate.* New York: Warner Books, 1988.

Leonard, George. *Adventures in Monogamy: Exploring the Creative Possibilities of Love, Sexuality, and Commitment.* New York: St. Martin's Press, 1988.

Lowen, Alexander. *Love, Sex, and Your Heart.* New York: Macmillan, 1988.

POINTS TO REMEMBER/THINGS TO DO

1. Try to put value judgments aside and look at this topic in terms of its affect on your achievement.
2. Consider how your romantic/sex life affects your profession.
3. Consider how your profession affects your romantic/sex life.
4. Rate the extent to which *sex, money, and power* influence your professional balance.
5. Pick three ways that your romantic/sex life could make you more balanced.
6. Include romance/sex in discussions with your partner.
7. Listen for your partner's ideas, attitudes, and concerns about romance and sex.
8. Don't let popular news stories or books upset your balanced romantic/sex life.

MY SEX/ROMANCE INVENTORY

CASUAL SEX

My Experience/Exposure:

My Impressions/Opinions:

My Balanced Future:

ACQUAINTANCE SEX

My Experience/Exposure:

My Impressions/Opinions:

My Balanced Future:

SEX WITH A LOVER

My Experience/Exposure:

My Impressions/Opinions:

My Balanced Future:

SEX WITH MY SPOUSE

My Experience/Exposure:

My Impressions/Opinions:

My Balanced Future:

SEX AND ACHIEVEMENT

Write down your general ideas, plans, and opinions.

8

THE HEART OF ACHIEVEMENT

I am an evangelist about the importance of maintaining a healthy heart. After I left graduate school and entered the workforce, I was deeply impressed by the number of heart attacks and strokes in the workplace. I saw successful, talented people giving their all to make it in the corporate world. They were doing great on that level, but their lives too often came to a sudden end.

I couldn't get over the nagging feeling that something was missing in the way we were going about our professional lives. I feel strongly now that success at work really does depend in part on the health of the body. People are strangling their achievement by not caring for their bodies. Those first images of seeing good employees being wheeled out of the front lobby, never to return to the work they had dedicated so much energy to, will always be etched in my mind.

Our hearts beat more than 104,000 times each day and we take for granted that they will continue doing it for "four score and ten." However, 1.5 million Americans every year have a heart attack, and one-third of these unfortunate ones do not live to talk about it or to get a chance at making some lifestyle changes.

I've been accused of scaring people with my warnings about heart attacks. We were once requested to change the name of a workshop from "Heart Attack Prevention" to "Heart Health" to avoid frightening people away. I'm still not sure whether gentle warnings or the cold, hard facts are more effective in getting people to take action to prevent heart disease in their lives.

A heart attack is not always a tragedy, because there is the possibility of full or almost full recovery afterward. Many people not only survive, but make radical changes in their lives that improve their overall health and even that of their families.

I want you to make some choices about your heart. These choices should be strategically made to add to your achievement. If you make the correct choices and make them as early as possible, you can harness the power of inertia to maintain your heart's health.

INERTIA AND WILL POWER

Most people change directions one or more times during the first few years in the workforce. Few people make major career changes after ten to fifteen years in the same field. The word that describes a person's reluctance to make major changes after several years is *inertia*.

Inertia is the force that keeps you doing the same thing year after year. Whether it is a good or a bad habit, inertia will keep it going unless something major happens that forces you to change against your will.

Most of us think that *will power* is the secret to accomplishing difficult goals like new health habits. We associate will power with struggle and sacrifice. This mythical force is often blamed for failure or credited for success, when in reality a combination of simple actions were put together for a purpose. These seeable and touchable things are exercise, planning, nutrition, goal setting, stress management, and all of the other aspects of Careerstyle. The most powerful way to get all of these concrete things into your life is to make use of the power of inertia—habits that keep themselves going once they're established. In other words, inertia can be a substitute for will power or, if you form harmful habits, can work against your having any will power available to you at all.

The health habits that you formed years ago have long since created their own inertia, and continue to affect the state of your cardiovascular system. Your job is to form habits that keep your heart healthy, and to practice these new habits long enough and often enough to give you the advantage of inertia.

There are many factors that influence how well your heart will perform. Each of these needs to be studied and considered for your own case. When you have decided on their value and your unique and personal way of using each factor, then you will be ready to incorporate them in your lifestyle. You will be one of the privileged few who avoid fads by sifting through new information and selecting the parts that have lasting value for your lifetime.

TABOOS AND MYTHICAL FORCES

Heart attack, along with sex, power, and money, is one of those semi-taboo subjects. Young people don't think it has anything to do with them, and older people do not want to be scared. Stay with me: If you're young, you're in luck! You have the option of acquiring information and habits that will keep your heart young and healthy. If you are more mature and have a tendency to avoid confronting your fears, remember that knowing about something tends to remove fear and create useful new attitudes.

I named this chapter "The Heart of Achievement" because each human being has a body and each body is fed, nourished, timed, and regulated by a heart. The human heart is truly at the center of all achievement, symbolically and literally. People with malfunctioning hearts or diseased cardiovascular systems have to live with restricted possibilities and reduced energy for working toward their goals.

This chapter is not meant to be a medical treatise on the heart or related diseases. The purpose is to give you evidence to support the claim that how you live affects your heart and that the state of your heart affects your ability to achieve. The references to research should pique your interest so that you educate yourself further on the functioning of the heart.

Make it a point to open a dialogue with your doctor. Let him or her know you want to take responsibility for your heart health. Physicians are busy, but good ones take the time to answer your questions and make lifestyle recommendations. One problem is that too many people take poor care of themselves and don't take responsibility for their health or even their happiness. You'll be surprised at the care and attention your physician can offer when you take the time to do your part.

THE CARDIOVASCULAR SYSTEM

The healthy cardiovascular system does its work with efficiency. The heart, lungs, arteries, veins, and capillaries are in a continual state of exchanging fresh oxygen for carbon dioxide gas and other waste products. The heart—the focal point of this system—determines how efficiently this exchange takes place.

The well-conditioned person has a cardiovascular system that delivers oxygen to body tissues with minimal effort. The unconditioned person has a system that must work much harder and faster during all stages of physical and emotional arousal, and even at rest.

Dr. Kenneth Cooper, the father of the aerobics school of thought, defines three types of hearts. The first is the unconditioned heart that beats faster at rest, at play, at work, and during any phase of any activity. This heart is of normal size and weight.

The second is the abnormally enlarged or diseased heart. This one may be larger in size, but the amount of work performed is no greater than the regular unconditioned heart. Externally it seems larger, but internally the chambers have no increased ability to pump blood throughout the body.

The third type is also enlarged but for a different reason. This heart looks larger and it does more work while pumping less. It is usually the heart of the well-conditioned person or athlete. As a result of consistently being exercised, this third type of heart has grown in size, increased in efficiency, beats slower at rest, and peaks at a lower and safer top end or "red line."

If you've read about autopsies of well-conditioned athletes that showed that the heart was somewhat enlarged, this is not an excuse to avoid changing your lifestyle to incorporate healthy habits. Athletes in good condition have well-developed heart muscle which can result in an enlarged heart. And even wonderfully fit atheletes may have underlying medical problems that can cause death. That is why medical check-ups are recommended and family history is so important.

The well-conditioned heart has spent lots of time in a high-achieve-ment phase called the *training zone*. This phase is entered when the heart is required to beat at a moderate to high level for about 20 to 30 minutes straight. The activities that accomplish this are called *aerobic* activities. This kind of exercise involves the large-muscle groups, requires deep breathing, and burns a good amount of fat.

To get the training effect on your heart, you need to do aerobic exercise of some sort for 20 to 30 minutes at least three times a week. You will not do your heart a favor, however, if you suddenly launch into an overvigorous aerobics program, or if you exercise sporadically. Study after study suggests that people who consistently exercise aerobically have fewer and less severe heart attacks than those who never exercise or those who go overboard sporadically.

Heart disease is the number one killer in the U.S. Each year over 1.5 million Americans have heart attacks, and more than 500,000 die as a result. A man has a one in five chance of dying of heart disease before he reaches sixty. Smokers develop heart disease three to six times more often than nonsmokers. Lack of consistent and moderate physical exercise about doubles one's chances of a fatal coronary. With these statistics, anyone considering a balanced lifestyle and prolonged achievement must include effective ways of protecting the efficiency of the heart.

To understand why aerobic exercise and other healthy habits are so important, let's look at heart attacks more closely.

BLOCKED OXYGEN SUPPLIES

The heart muscle or myocardium requires a consistent supply of oxygen. Aside from pumping oxygen to other parts of the body, the heart actually supplies its own oxygen through the coronary arteries. The system breaks down when the coronary arteries begin to slowly clog up with plaque, or fatty deposits. These little bits and pieces, atheromas, begin to accumulate and constrict the flow of blood within the artery, and efficiency begins to decrease. The term *arteriosclerosis* is used to describe this thickening or hardening of artery walls.

A chronic buildup can eventually have devastating effects, but another complication often occurs suddenly. A blood clot, or *thrombus,* can lodge itself in the already narrowed artery and severely restrict or completely cut off the flow of blood. When this happens in the brain, a stroke results, and a clot in the heart is called a *coronary thrombosis.*

When the blood supply to the heart tissue is severely reduced, some of the tissue dies, and this is called a *myocardial infarction*—that is, the death of heart tissue. Because the heart muscle cannot get the oxygen to do its job, it goes into a seizure that we call a heart attack.

An unfortunate error made by many is that at the onset of a heart attack pain may be felt, but as the muscle dies some of the pain subsides. It is a fatal mistake to assume that as the pain goes away so does the risk of heart damage and sudden death.

CORONARY RISK FACTORS

There are several statistical links found among people who have coronary heart disease. The term *risk factors* applies to genetic traits, family history, and lifestyle activities that correlate with incidence of heart disease. The most common risk factors are heredity, smoking, stress, high blood pressure, high cholesterol levels, obesity, lack of exercise, and diets high in saturated fats.

Our bodies are very resilient, and we can abuse them tremendously and still get away with it for the short term. Sooner or later, however, just when we require the most intense and prolonged efforts, the years of poor habits will take their toll.

Although some areas are out of our control—genetics and family history—many of the risk factors can be handled with lifestyle changes. The famous Framingham study found that sedentary men were much more likely to suffer from sudden and often fatal heart attacks. Many studies cite contradictory findings, but basically, studies demonstrate that consistent and vigorous exercise along with good dietary habits and stress management lead to a decreased incidence of coronary heart disease. Some may prefer to wait for absolute, water-tight cause-and-effect studies that prove that lifestyle habits affect the heart, but the prudent achiever knows that enough evidence leaning in one direction is worth considering, particularly when survival itself is at stake. The Pascalian Bet was one intelligent man's way of dealing with uncertainty.

LE PARI PASCALIEN (THE PASCALIAN BET)

The 17th century French philosopher Blaise Pascal died at age 39. Before his early death, he earned a place as one of the greatest minds in history. He discovered mathematics at age 12. He invented a calculating machine and a wristwatch and made them commercially available. He is credited with creating the modern literary French language and formulating the methods of the inductive method of scientific research. He would contemplate mathematical theories as a diversion for a toothache.

His "Pascalian Bet" involves belief or disbelief in God. He said that man's first choice is not to believe in God, but this choice leaves no chance for a future life. The other option is to believe, and if by chance there is a God—hallelujah, you made it...if not, you have lost nothing. Pascal thought it seemed a lot safer to believe and at least have a chance than to disbelieve and eliminate the possibility. And so it goes with the lifestyle changes you can make to improve your heart health.

If Pascal were here today, he'd probably buy a bicycle, eat good meals, and watch his stress level. It's a sound Pascalian Bet.

MEDICAL SOLUTIONS

When preventive approaches don't work, innovative medical procedures must be used. Today, some of the most brilliant medical minds are actively correcting existing problems and searching for preventive solutions. There is genuine good news for heart patients in the medical area. Here are some of the exciting and promising research developments.

Over $2 billion is paid out annually for bypass surgery. This technique is expensive, controversial, and a life saver. Up to now, four out of five bypass patients have been men. My guess is that this ratio will reach a 50-50 male-to-female split in the 1990s. The surgery involves bypassing a blocked artery with a vein or artery from another part of the body so that the heart gets its needed supply of oxygenated blood. Celebrities who have had the procedure include Milton Berle, Danny Kaye, Burt Lancaster, Barbara Bel Geddes (Dynasty), Alexander Haig, and Peggy Lee.

Several new developments, such as genetically engineered t-PA (tissue plasminogen activator), the protein that breaks down blood clots, are getting federal approval and rapid acceptance.

FEWER BYPASSES IN THE FUTURE

There is an alternative to bypass surgery called *angioplasty*. In this procedure, a balloon-tipped catheter is snaked through a blood vessel into the part of the heart where there is a blockage. The balloon is then inflated so that it literally breaks up the obstruction.

Other common reactive methods of lessening the effect of a heart attack use enzymes such as streptokinase and urokinase. These actually break down the clot once it has formed. The negatives are either the expense involved or excessive bleeding. Urokinase, in particular, has been successfully attached to antibodies that selectively destroy the clot without causing excessive bleeding. Tissue plasminogen activator (t-PA) also successfully breaks down clots in coronary arteries. It dramatically increases survival rates when given intravenously as soon as possible after a heart attack. Other researchers have attempted to use lasers in the removal of plaque from the coronary arteries.

CATCH IT QUICK

A cardiologist once told me that he believed that someday there would be a drug that would simply prevent coronary heart disease. Mixing wish with prediction, he said that people, probably young people, would perhaps drink a liquid in a small vial and it would protect them from the onset of the killer disease.

Meanwhile, until we find the wonder drug, the entire medical profession is pleading with us to change our lifestyles. Medical researchers are still searching for the magical remedy. Our part is to develop disease-reducing lifestyle habits and to help the medical profession with early diagnosis. Our lifestyle habits will not solve 100% of the coronary epidemic. Regular check-ups and early diagnosis of warning signals can be a great help.

500 BILLION CIGARETTES

The habit of smoking cigarettes has more inertia behind it than drinking alcohol and poor eating habits combined. Enemies are made by even mentioning smoking in a negative way, but there are some things that must be presented. Americans buy a lot of cigarettes. Cigarettes are implicated in a lot of heart attacks. Some doctors say that the single most important thing people can do to live longer is to stop smoking. Findings show that smokers who quit reduce the chance of having a heart attack dramatically. One of the surgeon general's warnings periodically rotated on cigarette packages says that "Quitting smoking now greatly reduces serious risk to your health."

The big news is that two years after quitting, the ex-smoker's risk of heart attack is almost the same as those who have never smoked. Not a bad trade-off. Of course lung cancer is a different story and depends on the total number of years and the amount smoked. Other research has found that it takes even more than two years of not smoking before the risk of heart attack returns to that of those who never smoked. If you are a smoker, this information can be a good motivator to do something about the habit, especially if you have other risk factors in your family history or medical profile. Face it, we all make daily choices that translate into success or failure, good times or bad times.

The consumption of over a half trillion cigarettes a year supports a large industry. This is the same industry that has received highest honors for their creativity and effectiveness in world-wide advertising effectiveness. The "Marlboro Man" ads are right up at the top of the all-time classic and effective ad campaigns, along with the Volkswagon Beetle ads and the "I'd like to give the world a Coke" campaign. Persuasive advertising plays on tradition, inertia, and the need for a positive self-image to make us start smoking, try a new brand, or keep smoking the same "favorites."

FISH, SIDE ROADS, AND EXCITEMENT

A final note on three positive findings that you may find useful in your own preventive program. First, it seems that eating fish may have an effect in preventing coronary heart disease. Eskimos have a diet that is high in fat, but they don't have the expected high incidence of heart disease. The solution to this mystery is that Eskimos eat a lot of fish that live in deep, cold water, and these fish contain a special type of unsaturated (Omega-3) fat.

Unsaturated fats are the ones that dieticians have been urging us to use in place of saturated fats—those that become hard at room temperature. The super-unsaturated fats found in deep-sea fish are thought to keep them from freezing in the cold water. This anti-freeze effect may assist in thinning the blood and preventing clots. In addition, Omega-3 fats reduce serum cholesterol and triglicerides and increase high-density lipoprotein levels (HDL), all of which has a positive effect on reducing heart disease. No one should wait for miracles, but every little bit helps in your strategy for healthy balance.

Another piece of good news is that the body has some ability to avoid cardiac infarction, or heart tissue death, in the event of a heart attack, by using *collateralization* or "side roads." Many heart-attack victims survive and recover thanks to a system of secondary capillaries (branches of arteries) that feed the heart muscle that has been cut off by a clogged coronary artery. It is thought that consistent exercise contributes to the development of these lifesaving side roads. This collateral circulation will not prevent a heart attack, but in the event you have one, some of your heart muscle will not die from complete oxygen starvation.

Here again the Pascalian Bet may be helpful. Eating more fish and exercising well may or may not reduce the chance of having a heart attack. They may or may not help you recover once you have already suffered one. My money is on the side that says it's worth the chance.

The third piece of good news has to do with the effect of exercise on the side-effects of getting excited. When we are excited, under emotional stress, or in any way "pumped up," our adrenal glands start secreting hormones throughout the system. The unconditioned heart responds with fits and starts. It palpitates, skips beats, and generally makes a mess of our equilibrium. The conditioned heart is prepared to handle the extra juice without getting overly excited and beating wildly. This shows that your system is fine tuned and very efficient. It can respond quickly when needed and stays under control when excited. It's this kind of control that the high achiever needs for a lifetime of consistent productivity.

The well-rounded professional usually has a gut feel for what is right. This usually means selecting the option that is long term, strategic, and reasonable. Lifestyle changes that affect the cardiovascular system can help turn the unconditioned heart into the heart of the balanced achiever.

111

FOR FURTHER READING

American Medical Association. *Home Medical Advisor.* New York: Random House, 1988.

Cooper, Kenneth, M.D. *Aerobics.* New York: M. Evans and Company, 1968.

Samuels, Mike, M.D., and Nancy Samuels. *The Well Adult: The Complete Guide to Protecting and Improving Your Health.* New York: Summit Books, 1988.

Whitaker, Julian M., M.D. *Reversing Heart Disease: A Vital Program to Prevent, Treat, and Eliminate Cardiac Problems Without Surgery.* New York: Warner Books, 1985.

POINTS TO REMEMBER/THINGS TO DO

1. Get medical advice and attention before starting to exercise or when you have health concerns.
2. Your heart "dislikes" any sudden changes in lifestyle or exercise intensity.
3. All of your achievement depends on your heart's health.
4. Heart attacks are common but preventable.
5. Smoking, dieting, poor nutrition, and sedentary lifestyles are linked to heart attacks.
6. You can find research statistics to support *anything* you believe (or want to believe).
7. Aside from medical/genetic conditions, we have control of our heart health.
8. The personal and business costs of preventing heart attacks are a fraction of the costs associated with damaged hearts.

MY CARDIOVASCULAR INVENTORY

	Yes	Maybe/ Sometimes	No
1. I get regular medical check-ups.	☐	☐	☐
2. I get specific heart check-ups.	☐	☐	☐
3. My diet is balanced.	☐	☐	☐
4. I get moderate exercise.	☐	☐	☐
5. I get consistent exercise.	☐	☐	☐
6. My stress is controlled.	☐	☐	☐
7. My cholesterol level is okay.	☐	☐	☐
8. I relax regularly.	☐	☐	☐
9. My family is free of heart disease*.	☐	☐	☐
10. My life is paced well.	☐	☐	☐

---

8 – 10 Yes's = Keep it up!
　　5 – 7 = OK, but not very safe.
Under 5 = Very risky. Make changes and see your doctor.

Genetic (hereditary) factors alone can play a major role in the possibility of having heart disease.

9

WHAT TO DO ABOUT STRESS

Some thrive on it, some die from it, and still others just quit. Stress comes in many forms and people react to it in their own particular way. In this chapter we'll cover recognizing the signs of stress, finding the causes, and doing something about it, then explore what factors make stress fatal for some and a source of creativity for others.

Our personal responsibility is to learn to manage the stress in our lives on a daily basis as well as over the long term. You must first learn to recognize your personal signs of stress, then pinpoint the suspected causes, and finally learn to manage it in such a way that you thrive on it, rather than living a life so risk-free that you avoid it, or letting it take over your life to such a degree that you may even die from it.

DEFINING STRESS

One definition of stress is "the body's reaction to conditions that make demands on it." The word literally means "to draw tight." In his original work on stress management, Dr. Hans Selye describes it as "the non-specific response of the body to any demand placed upon it," that is, the body's heightened state of readiness in response to some taxing condition.

Cognitive psychologists say that *perceived* demands have as much effect on the body's stress responses as do circumstances—that what goes on inside of the mind has as much potential for stress as physical attacks from the outside. In other words, if we just think something is frightening,

115

it will be stressful. Stress is not the event itself, but our mental and physical reactions to what's going on around us.

No one knows why humans respond differently to similar circumstances. If you slapped ten total strangers in the face, you will, of course, get strong reactions; the variety of responses would be the only surprise. After being struck for no apparent reason, one or two would slap back, one might kick you, another would sock you, one would tear your throat out, while still others would blush, turn, and run. Reactions to any cause of stress can be just as varied.

The ability to recognize stress may be one of the best defenses against the harm it can do. If you recognize it early, you can actually turn it into something positive.

GENERAL ADAPTATION SYNDROME

Experts on stress use a model called the General Adaptation Syndrome to describe the stages of alarm, resistance, and exhaustion that a person goes through in reaction to stress. *Alarm* is the stage at which you consciously or subconsciously become aware that something is placing a demand on you. *Resistance* is the phase during which you attempt to fight off the stress and return your body and mind to normal functioning. If this phase lasts too long, you will enter the *exhaustion* phase, in which the body and mind begin to break down.

Stress management seems to stay in fashion. There are seminars and workshops on regular stress, executive stress, family stress, "eustress" (that's the good kind), teenage stress, and stress in Silicon Valley. Other popular seminar topics like assertiveness, neurolinguistic programming, and Quality Circles have lost the public's attention or have been modified and repackaged, but stress management seems to be so needed in contemporary life that it has not lost its audience. My guess is that future research on stress management will break the topic down into more specific categories rather than lumping all unexplained anxiety into one broad category.

THE GOOD LIFE AND STRESS

Believe it or not, the great things that happen to you also cause stress. Researchers have found increased levels of stress-related chemicals (adreno-corticotropic hormone, or ACTH) in the bloodstream following both negative and positive situations.

Furthermore, the chemicals remain in the bloodstream long after your conscious awareness of the stress has passed. You may have forgotten about how excited you were, but your body is still dealing with a massive dose of various mood-altering chemicals, and has no way of knowing whether the adrenalin racing through your system is from a disaster or from winning a lottery. The result is that your body has an urgent need to bring things back into equilibrium, and while it's fixing things, you may feel exhausted, frustrated, or even depressed.

Not much has been said or written about the positive life events that result in stress reactions. Getting a raise often means higher expectations of your performance. Getting married involves money, family, and a host of other potentially stressful problems. A new car means payments, insurance, and possible vandalism. Most of these positive events in our lives include an element of change and uncertainty.

There is no conclusive proof, but change and uncertainty seem to be at the root of most anxiety-producing situations in our lives. It's no wonder we resist change more often than we accept it gracefully. When change is positive, we still feel that twinge of anxiety. The chemical results are present regardless of the nature of the event. Your body and mind will take time to recover and bring your system back into a fine-tuned equilibrium.

A BAD RAP

Stress has quite a dubious reputation. It's needed to perform, but it causes heart attacks. It's the competitive edge, but Type A behavior will kill you. Stress keeps us motivated, yet debilitates; it's even thought to be a cause of bad breath.

117

For some professionals, there's a big payoff to retaining a high level of stress in their lives. They may brag about being in a fast-paced and stressful job, or wear it as a badge of loyalty on their chest to impress an employer or spouse. The payoff—pats on the back, sighs of sympathy, and outright pity—are the little rewards they have become accustomed to because of their "heavy load." They get caught in the spiral trap of believing that they get this sympathetic treatment because they endure all that stress without complaining or rebelling.

The truth is that these individuals know very little about stress recognition or stress management. Unchecked stress is inconsistent with high achievement, and top performers also know that if they remain in an unhealthy and stressful environment without changing it, their performance will go down. Some stress will motivate you to higher levels of performance, but it must be monitored to remain useful and keep you vibrant.

RECOGNIZING STRESS: "IT'S IN THE BODY"

You probably already know something about how to spot the telltale signs of stress in people around you, but it's sometimes harder to recognize them in yourself. To start with, you will almost always notice a change in your body. It may be sporadic at first and then progress to a persistent and embarrassing eye twitch, stutter, bowel malfunction, sore neck and back, headaches, or rash. It may show up as a change in your eating or sleeping patterns, your sexual energy, or your heart rate.

EATING

What you eat and how you eat can actually be a cause of stress itself, or your eating habits may be altered as a consequence of some anxiety. You may notice that you're skipping meals or snacking excessively when you normally limit yourself to three meals a day. If instead of the occasional craving for a pizza or ice cream, you find yourself at the pizza parlor or the ice cream shop five days a week, you should take inventory of what may be bothering you before you gain fifty pounds and make yourself sick.

If you notice a change in your scale weight without dieting or altering your exercise habits, watch out! Something is on your mind and you may not even know it.

Sound eating habits prepare you to fight off stress, while poor eating habits can be a direct cause of stress. The point here is that any change in your eating patterns can be an accurate signal that there is conflict in your life.

SLEEPING

A change in your sleeping patterns can indicate that your mind and body are struggling with a heavy load. You may not even know that there *is* a conflict in your life. Your first sign may be that you find yourself lying awake at 3:00 a.m. noticing the funny little cracks in the ceiling. Some part of your mind continues to hammer away at the conflict while you think you are going to hit the sack and sleep soundly. Alternatively, you may need much more rest than usual, and you find yourself falling asleep waiting for a red light to change.

Disrupted sleep patterns may mean that you are very excited or very upset about something. A new job or living situation will normally result in a mild sleep disruption, and a deteriorating love relationship can be expected to disturb anyone's sleep. Other life changes may not be as easy to identify, but they disturb your sleep habits just the same.

Sleep disturbances can be useful in getting at the cause of stress. If your sleeping patterns have suddenly changed, begin by keeping a log of the number of times you wake up during the night or when you feel exhausted during the day. The next step is to look for patterns and probable causes. Later in this chapter we will go into various ways of narrowing the field of stressor suspects.

SEXUAL FUNCTIONING

It can be confusing and unnerving when your sex life gets disrupted. Although there are many possible physical and mental causes for sexual dysfunction, one of the most probable is stress. Any sudden change in your sexual appetite or functioning may be a flag indicating some sort of stress or conflict in your life that happened to surface under the covers.

If your sexual patterns are already varied, it will be tough to distinguish a true change that results from stress. For example, suppose you're knocking yourself out at work to rebuild sagging field sales, and you find that you're routinely telling your spouse or lover that you're too tired to make love. You might be simply emotionally exhausted, or you might be entertaining serious doubts about whether you are capable of pulling sales up. The stress of your self-doubt may be what's *really* undermining your sex life.

In Chapter 7 we discussed how sex and achievement can reinforce each other or foul each other up. If stress is interfering with your sex life, your achievement is sure to be affected by the additional worries that sexual dysfunction or disinterest create.

PULSE RATE

As your stress level rises, your body goes on alert, causing changes in your digestion, circulation, and heart rate. The easiest to observe is your heart rate. If you are very observant and in tune with your body, changes in digestion and circulation will be apparent, but your heart rate can be measured at any time in less than one minute.

When you are under stress, your heart rate as measured in beats per minute (bpm) usually goes up. If you are already familiar with using your pulse rate to manage your exercise program, you will quickly notice the effects of stress. If you don't know what your pulse rate is and should be, read the chapters on exercise and heart health and learn to take your pulse and interpret it.

MIND GAMES

Funny things happen to your mind when the stresses and strains of life catch up with you. No, you're not going crazy—you just may be under some heavy stress without even recognizing it. We have already discussed the variety of ways your body signals you to lighten up a bit. The mind can play just as many tricks when conflicts in your life persist over a period of time.

Fantasizing. Fantasies are a normal and healthy part of the well-adjusted personality. They're a great way to safely live out some otherwise taboo activities, and even provide relief for minor stress. Some fantasies may give you a touch of guilt or embarrassment, but that's better than getting injured or arrested. One sign of stress buildup is that fantasies may become annoying and produce more anxiety than they eliminate.

Dreams. Sleep scientists tell us that everyone dreams from one to two hours each night, sometimes in black and white, and sometimes in living color. I have friends who can remember every detail of their dreams. They can recall the exact colors, textures, smells, and sensations. On the other hand, I can barely remember that I dreamed at all. If I think about what is on my mind as soon as I wake up, I can often place bits and pieces together like a puzzle or a slide show. When I'm under stress, I remember more of my dreams. The scenes of being chased, scared, or missing elusive goals are much more vivid than my normal dreams.

Many people can tell that their dream patterns change when conflicts during the daylight hours are not worked out. Freud said that our dreams are manifestations of our fears, wishes, and inhibitions. It stands to reason that changes in our dream patterns are another one of the signposts we can use to recognize that stress has been mounting.

Subvocal Ruminations. Subvocal ruminations include the song you can't get out of your mind, that stupid joke or jingle that keeps popping up, or the phrase that keeps coming into your consciousness. These silent repetitions of a few words or sentences tend to appear while you are trying to sleep, concentrate, or relax. You're under stress when you notice that these annoying ruminations keep interrupting your normal pattern of thought or your attempts at clearing your mind.

Subvocal ruminations are not spoken, but they are clearly "heard" in your mind. This sign of stress is overlooked by most people as just a strange inconvenience that somehow goes away in time. I once missed an entire night of sleep tossing and turning while the lines of a popular song persisted in running through my mind. It practically drove me crazy! I used to like the song, but now it only brings back memories of a very stressful time in my life.

Lost Train of Thought. Losing your train of thought can be yet another sign of stress. The dictionary defines *non sequitur* literally as "does not follow," or a conclusion that does not fit the premises upon which it was based. This gap in the stream of reasoning is joked about as a sign of senility or being absent-minded. Everyone loses their train of thought at some time. One of the most embarrassing moments in life can be losing one's train of thought in the middle of a presentation or speaking engagement, an experience that can bring up an intense desire to change careers or crawl into a hole.

Even if one of these embarrassing incidents hasn't happened to you, you may sometimes find yourself coming up with "non sequiturs" more often than usual. Your thinking gets jumbled, and you have a hard time maintaining your concentration—thinking about one thing for more than a minute becomes as hard as running a marathon.

Accidents and Mistakes. As a youngster you may have broken a vase or a bowl to get adult attention. Hopefully you grew out of that stage, but psychologists tell us that grown men and women sometimes do equally crazy things to get attention or to get even. Frequent accidents and mistakes are a sign of stress. Stress causes a preoccupation with several things at once. On the one hand, we're trying to conduct business as usual, and on the other, we're trying to correct the problem. As our attention span shortens due to the stress, we become prone to a continual series of mistakes and accidents. This is why we're cautioned not to drive when emotionally upset or very angry: pressure often leads to poor judgment and sudden mishaps.

FALSE ALARMS

Be careful not to become paranoid. Every little change in your life does not signal unresolved conflict that leads to stress. Many other things can cause sleepless nights, sexual dysfunction, or mental lapses. Medications, hormonal changes, and even heavy exercise can all result in signals identical to those resulting from stress. For example, if you suffer from premenstrual syndrome (PMS), you can expect stress-like effects in your daily life pattern. A vigorous workout of racquet-ball, handball, or aerobics may affect your appetite and sleep patterns, but these changes have nothing to do with stress. The difference is that these "false alarms" can be spotted and controlled very easily.

NABBING THE CULPRIT

After you have identified stress in your life, it may or may not be clear where it came from. If you just got fired, won a major contract, or broke off a long-term relationship, you'll easily identify the source of your problems. You may have an elevated pulse rate and keep losing your train of thought. Another person might have a voracious appetite and lose all sexual desire. In both situations, you'd immediately know what was going on.

But what if it's not so clear-cut? You may suddenly notice that you have been nervous all day and your appetite has about disappeared. In addition to that, you've made some rather stupid mistakes lately—the kind that make you think you killed some brain cells at that last party. For the life of you, you cannot figure out what's causing it. Your first action should be to rule out any stress "false alarms." After you have eliminated medications, monthly hormonal changes, cuts and bruises, food poisoning, and heavy exercise as the source, you begin the process of finding the real stressor in your life.

These hidden stress producers are the most dangerous, because they linger on and on without being attacked head on. The symptoms of unidentified stress—headaches, mistakes, food binges, and so on—may be masked by alcohol, drugs, eating disorders, or even suicide.

Check for associations in time, place, or similarity that may be causing the stress.

ISOLATING THE GUILTY VARIABLE

What we will call the "guilty variable" is usually referred to by researchers as the "independent variable." Experimental scientists look for causal relationships, that is, the factor that causes a certain effect. If causal relationships can be identified, it becomes possible to predict and control circumstances or behavior. If you can isolate the guilty variable that's causing your stress, you will come a step closer to predicting when you will be under its influence, so that you can avoid those circumstances or make allowance for the effects. You can determine whether or not you have enough control to tackle it, change it, or accept it.

This next section will suggest several areas to examine when you are trying to isolate the probable cause of your stress reaction. You may have your own additions to the list of potential culprits.

TIME OF DAY

When stress seems to come and go, try to determine whether it occurs primarily in the morning or afternoon. Just identifying mornings or afternoons as high-stress times of the day will bring you a lot closer to nailing it down. Many people dread the morning hours because of uncertainty at the office or unpleasant meetings held before lunch. Others find the afternoons high in stress and notice that they have a real distaste for the calls, errands, or disturbances that usually occur in the late afternoon.

DAY OF WEEK/WEEK OF MONTH

More heart attacks occur on Mondays than on the other days of the work week. As far as I know, no one knows why, but you can guess that it may be a result of abuse of the body over the weekend or the strain of beginning another week of work. Finding your personal stress day or week could be as simple as rating each day from one to ten for three weeks. You may find that Wednesdays turn out to be high stress days with an average score of eight and Mondays only have a score of three (one being low stress and ten being high stress). The last week of the month is a tough one for many because of bills coming due and work deadlines.

LOCATION

Some men I know get sweaty palms just thinking about shopping for groceries. Mention shopping for clothes and they almost faint. For these fellows, large stores seem to spell stress. Of course, sex stereotypes rarely hold water, but many women feel extremely uncomfortable going to a car dealership, even to just look at the new models from a distance.

We all know people who won't set foot in an airplane, or who are willing to climb fifteen flights of stairs rather than take an elevator. In a way, these people are lucky because they know what causes their stress. On a less dramatic scale, each of us probably has a couple of locations we would rather avoid. If you can identify them by trial and error, deduction, or keeping notes, you'll be able to avoid some of the stress in day-to-day life. I particularly recommend note-taking, because I've noticed that when you spend a few minutes writing down your impressions, hidden feelings often come to the surface.

SPECIAL ACTIVITIES

Weddings, business lunches, funerals, and parties may have special significance for you. Because of your position, your relatives, or your business connections, you may be required to attend all of these types of functions. Your role as business person, head of household, or just plain "tough guy" might make it hard for you to show emotions or admit that you hate the activity. This type of bottling up is part of the

Little-Big Boy Syndrome, where men learn at an early age to act like big boys and keep feelings inside. This is a definite cause of stress.

It is sometimes difficult for men and women to step outside their roles long enough to pinpoint the special activities that give them trouble and create stress. One big clue is that you feel amazingly relieved after certain events—watch for that big sigh of relief after specific activities.

Some feel performance pressure in love relationships and cannot wait for intimate activities to be over. Or you might feel extremely relieved after business lunches, because for you they have a high stress quotient. If you monitor your feelings and anxiety before, during, and after special activities, you may identify one of your personal stress producers.

PARTICULAR PEOPLE

People you openly dislike rarely cause you much stress. In fact, you may even relish nipping at their heels from time to time. Open warfare is less stressful than subtle sabotage. When your feelings are open and easily vented, the pressure does not build to a breaking point.

There may be others in your life that you love dearly, but strangely enough, every time you're around them, you notice your particular signs of stress. A parent, sibling, spouse, lover, or close friend may drive your stress level up a few notches.

With people close to you, the cause of stress may be unresolved conflict, competition, fear of failure, or loss of approval. Identifying the people in your life that cause you stress can be scary, but worth the end result. Many times, simply asking that person for clarification can clear up the problem, and you can come out of it with one less stressor in life.

Take time to analyze past relations with the person. Identify unresolved conflicts that both of you have been carrying around for months or even years. Try writing all the possibilities down and then eliminating the least likely ones. Take the ones that remain and rank them from the most to least likely culprits. The time spent will be worth it.

THRIVING, DYING, AND QUITTING

People respond to stress in three ways. Look around at your friends, associates, role models, and even your enemies. You'll find that most of them respond to sticky and stressful events by tackling them head on, or getting flattened by them, or by just plain dropping out of the race.

Everyone reacts differently to a fight. If an opponent is viewed as a hated and powerful enemy, you can either respond with a quick attack or take the midnight express out of town. If we view stress itself as an enemy, our responses will be less effective than if we consider the opportunity to discover something about ourselves or even to spur us on to a creative solution. Some people consistently use the stress in their lives to accomplish great tasks. These people view it as a challenge that can be dangerous, but they know it has many achievement possibilities as well.

Another response is that of those who either do not know the dangers of stress or do not care enough to do anything about it. These people will die young with a lot of money in the bank.

The last group can be called the quitting type. These are generally low achievers who would rather quit than fight or create anything new for themselves.

THRIVING ON STRESS

Some people—maybe you!—just love a challenge. These people take the roughest road, enjoy achievement, and generally root for the underdog. They'll turn on a baseball game and wait for the score in order to cheer for the team that is down. Many of the great athletes, actors, and entrepreneurs fit into this thriving group. They know the danger and the potential of stress. The big difference is that these people are masters at setting up their lives to take full advantage of the boosting power of stress and they also take responsibility for handling its negative consequences.

Once again, the first step is to give yourself a good diet and a sound exercise program. These two items keep cropping up in the well-balanced lifestyle. Those who thrive on stress do not go overboard into fanaticism. They simply know that from time to time it's okay to skimp on what they eat and on how well they exercise, but never during high-stress times. High-stress times separate the winners from the losers, and good eating and exercise habits give you a competitive edge when stress is a factor.

Those who thrive on stress tend to be good at creating a positive mental picture of a difficult situation. By making these positive mental resolutions, they seem to reaffirm their commitment to their long-term goals and to their power to eventually make things right. They usually manage to resolve a stressful situation in the way they pictured it. Psychologists say that when we smile and when we focus on positive aspects of a problem, our breathing becomes deeper and our tolerance for frustration takes a noticeable jump.

Those who use stress well tend to manage their daily hours well, and they refuse to fall into the trap of procrastination. They define their priorities, which helps them avoid spending time on useless activities that needlessly increase stress.

DYING FROM STRESS

A businessman brags about his "stretch" workday and how much he can accomplish. He has a morning breakfast meeting and then works until his lunch meeting. After his lunch session he cranks out more work and then goes to his dinner meeting. After this meeting he either goes back to work or takes work home to finish the loose ends. His stretch day had better accomplish a lot, because his chance of spending a few weeks in a hospital will be high if this routine continues.

Mental and emotional breakdowns occur when your stress and strain pass from the resistance phase into the exhaustion phase. The most common final straw comes from what is called the "multiplier effect." This is the stress equivalent of the person who uses drugs in addition to alcohol, and unfortunately finds that the effects of each are not added together but multiplied. People can handle amazing amounts of stress, confusion, and frustration. The breaking point comes when an added element of surprise multiplies the stress you have been handling so well. Mr. Stretch who is proud about how much he accomplishes without breaks will get nailed by something as simple as salt, coffee, alcohol, or some unexpected change in his environment.

Physicians estimate that over half of all medical complaints stem from psychological stress. Those who die from stress hardly ever take time to understand it. They rarely admit that it exists. Many who *do* understand—maybe even you, reading this chapter—feel that stress is a badge of achievement or sign of importance. It's easy to fall into the trap of complaining about how many hours or days we work without breaks or vacations. Any sympathy we get gives us a payoff that keeps us from finding solutions.

On the other hand, denying and repressing stress only leads to isolation and pain. Those who are likely to die from stress seldom open up about what's going on, much less express their feelings and cry. A first step would be to at least talk to a trusted friend. Many people in this category have not developed close friendships. If you recognize yourself here, your first step is to build casual relationships that can lead to closer and more intimate exchanges of feelings. Instead of blaming outside circumstances and using substitute solutions for the problem, you can gradually take steps to communicate your feelings and change your lifestyle.

QUITTING

Every college student remembers the semester when they registered for six classes and only had time for three. Each of us has to make adjustments when priorities change or new developments pop up. "Giving up" could simply mean a change of strategy or reassessment of your potential and your capabilities. Looked at from this perspective, quitting is not bad in itself unless it becomes a habitual response to problems. If you find this happening to you, quitting should be your absolute last resort. Your future good lifestyle habits may depend on this challenge in your life.

In our context of thriving, dying, and quitting we have the two extremes and the compromise. The high achievers use stress to build success. Stress-related fatalities are the result of extreme abuse and denial. The middle ground can be a comfortable alternative, and in fact all of us use it at different times. It may be rational and prudent to quit medical or law school, or it may be just a cheap way out.

Small business owners quit at an alarming rate. Some should never have started, but many just could not persevere through the stress. Getting out is fine if your capabilities in no way match the requirements or if your career ambitions are in a much different area. If, however, you are qualified and you want to accomplish the task, then quitting may be no more than avoidance of the discomforts of dealing with normal stress levels.

It is clear that any change—whether positive or negative—can cause conflict that leads to stress. Success itself increases your level of stress for several reasons. First of all, success calls for changes in your usual patterns and in your relationships. The new supervisor will take great pains to fit into the old group after a promotion. A happy couple enjoying a new relationship sense a strain in their other relations with friends and family.

The second reason success brings stress is that once you reach a certain level, you risk falling backwards. The pressure to maintain your success level is too much for some. They think that what goes up literally must come down. Unfortunately this self-fulfilling thought pattern causes them to back out and blame it on the stress of success.

Fear of failure influences most people at the beginning of a new job, relationship, or start-up venture. This fear of losing money or prestige, or of embarrassing oneself, is what makes most people avoid even starting a risky proposition. You have to start something before you can quit.

Some people develop a downward spiral of failure because they start many projects and then bail out when it looks like there may be trouble ahead. This reinforces their fear of risk because not only did their project not succeed, but they have to deal with the consequences of the stress of failing. Rather than gearing up with diet, exercise, time management, and positive mental resolutions like the thrivers do, this group cuts their losses and avoids any possibility of embarrassing failure.

Everyone should quit when a particular strategy or tactic is wrong. The very next step is to regroup and assertively attack another strategic goal. People who take this approach seldom wear the label of "quitter," but find themselves respected, fulfilled, and successful.

RELAX AND ACHIEVE

The high-achieving professional *must* learn to define and recognize their own personal signs of stress. If you create balance in your life as we have discussed throughout this book, a lot of unnecessary stress will be eliminated, and you'll be prepared to attack the essentials that fit nicely into your strategy of achievement. This strategy includes long-range, medium-range, and immediate goals. Your stress level will determine how many of these strategic milestones you meet and what other parts of your lifestyle will be disrupted along the way.

Early recognition of your personal signs and reactions to stress will clue you into a needed lifestyle adjustment. You may alter your eating, exercise, or support contacts. Your aim is to beef up whatever part of your Careerstyle will help you leverage your stress on your way to reaching the top of whatever ladder you are climbing.

You alone can decide how to balance your career, your professional life, and your body's health in ways that make stress a minor issue in your life.

FOR FURTHER READING

Benson, Herbert, M.D., and Miriam Klipper. *The Relaxation Response.* New York: William Morrow, 1975.

Davis, Martha, Elizabeth Robbins Eshelman, and Matthew Mckay. *The Relaxation and Stress Reduction Workbook.* Oakland, CA: New Harbinger Publications, 1988.

Kirsta, Alix. *The Book of Stress Survival: Identifying and Reducing Stress in Your Life.* New York: Simon & Schuster, 1986.

Lidell, Lucy. *The Sensual Body: The Ultimate Guide to Body Awareness and Self-Fulfillment.* New York: Simon & Schuster, 1987.

Mason, L. John. *Stress Passages: Surviving Life's Transitions Grace fully.* Berkeley, CA: Celestial Arts, 1988.

Potter, Beverly. *Preventing Job Burnout: Transforming Work Pressures into Productivity.* Los Altos, CA: Crisp Publications, 1987.

POINTS TO REMEMBER/THINGS TO DO

1. Stressful situations progress through *alarm, resistance,* and *exhaustion.*
2. List your personal signs of stress (stomach pain or nausea, soreness in your neck, accidents, over- or undereating, etc.).
3. Certain people, places, or things may trigger stress. List things that trigger stress reactions for you.
4. You can choose to *thrive* on stress, *die* from it, or just get out (*quit*).
5. Positive as well as negative events cause stress.
6. Stress results from your *reactions* to events rather than from the events themselves.

7. You can learn to handle amazing amounts of stress with enlightened management of your attitude, exercise program, diet, and lifestyle balance.
8. Avoid bragging about how much stress you handle or the long hours you work.
9. If you have consistently productive work days along with leisure and recreation, you will accomplish as much as if you work long hours, skip meals, and work weekends.

MY STRESS INVENTORY

MY PHYSICAL SIGNS

Eating more   _____
Eating less   _____
Junk food   _____
Odd times   _____
Sleeping more   _____
Sleeping less   _____
Trouble sleeping   _____
Sexual problems   _____
Racing pulse rate   _____
(   )   _____

MY MENTAL SIGNS

Fantasizing often   _____
Strange dreams   _____
Talking to myself   _____
Lose my train   _____
  of thought
More accidents   _____
More mistakes   _____
(   )   _____

WHEN AM I STRESSED?

Time of Day

Early Morning   _____
Late Morning   _____
Mid-day   _____
Early Afternoon   _____
Late Afternoon   _____
Early Evening   _____
Late Evening   _____

Day of Week

Mondays   _____
Tuesdays   _____
Wednesdays   _____
Thursdays   _____
Fridays   _____
Saturdays   _____
Sundays   _____

Locations

Home   _____
Office   _____
Stores   _____
Buildings   _____
Automobile   _____
(   )   _____

Special Activities

Weddings   _____
Shopping   _____
Lunches   _____
Conventions   _____
Anniversaries   _____
(   )   _____

MY STRESS INVENTORY
(continued)
WHEN AM I STRESSED?

Certain People

		Holidays	
Father	_____	Christmas	_____
Mother	_____	Thanksgiving	_____
Spouse/lover	_____	Birthdays	_____
Sister	_____	New Year's	_____
Brother	_____	Halloween	_____
Boss	_____	Easter	_____
Friends	_____	Valentine's Day	_____
Co-worker	_____	Labor Day	_____
Children	_____	Fourth of July	_____
( )	_____	( )	_____

10

SUCCESS WITH PEOPLE

Dealing with people can be a pain in the neck or it can be the thing that most makes your life worth living. It's very tempting to fall into the trap of believing that if there are problems in our relationships with other people, it's because of how the other person is. We can tell great stories about how awful they are, and we can easily get our friends' sympathy for our belief that it's all the other person's fault. You probably know some extreme examples of this—people who are constantly telling you how impossible everyone around them is.

But I'll tell you a secret—you can create miracles in those difficult relationships if you change the way *you* are and get out of the trap of leaving the success or failure of the relationship solely in the other person's lap.

I once saw a bumper sticker that said: "Business is great—Life is wonderful—People are terrific." They call it a self-fulfilling prophecy, and the truth is that whether business will be great, life will be wonderful, and whether or not people really are that terrific depends on *you.*

EINSTEIN, SHAW, AND FREUD HAD TIME

When George Seldes was preparing the manuscript for *The Great Quotations* and *The Great Thoughts,* two works covering the thinking of famous and infamous men and women of history, he discovered something that surprised him. After writing to almost a hundred celebrated writers and thinkers asking them to check the accuracy of his interpretation of their work, only a few replied. Curiously enough, those who replied were people like Einstein,

Shaw, Freud, and Huxley, while the more minor celebrities, those who hadn't achieved lasting success, couldn't take the time to check their proofs. It was the great thinkers who took time to respond to someone else's request.

This chapter will give you some tips on how to demonstrate your genuine interest in other people—and if you follow them, they will pay off over and over, in both your personal and professional life.

Here are the basics of good people skills: return phone calls and letters promptly, remember people's names, learn how to really listen to them, and be a good networker—put people in touch with other people, and be prepared to exchange leads, ideas, and information.

This chapter also includes two sections that are vital to how you present yourself to others. Your public image and your leadership skills can either drive people away or make them beat a path to your office, cubicle, or front door. Let's begin with the telephone.

PICK UP THAT PHONE

I'm sure you've had the experience of trying to reach someone unsuccessfully—they just can't seem to return your phone calls, and when you finally reach them, they apologize and say they just didn't have time. It leaves you feeling that they must be much busier and more important than you are, and that you are a very low priority on their list of things to do. Even if you don't acknowledge it to yourself, you're less likely to stay in touch with this person, and they've lost at least a little part of your friendship.

If you are the person who's sloppy about returning phone calls, you know that it leaves you with a nagging feeling of guilt—maybe that call was important, or maybe that person will be irritated with you for not responding.

This is one of the easiest people skills you can learn—pick up the phone and clear up all your phone messages. You don't have to settle down to a long afternoon's chat, but give them your full attention for a few minutes, resolve their need, say a friendly goodbye that leaves them feeling good, and clear your mind of that little bit of incompletion. It leaves you with more energy for the priority things on your list, and it may turn up the business lead of your life!

Later in this chapter we're going to talk about your appearance. Interestingly enough, the way you look even affects how you are on the phone—your confidence, your spontaneity, and even your negotiating skills.

The principle of keeping up to date on your communication also applies to written communication. Respond promptly to memos, personal letters, and social invitations. One way to save time on minor communications is to write a response on the memo itself, make a copy for your files, and send the original back to the sender.

Be sure to personalize your communication when it's appropriate. Everyone loves reading personal messages referring to their children or the last time you saw each other. Many successful professionals keep the names of spouses and children in their address book specifically so they can refer to them in letters and phone calls—they know that the personal interest this shows pays off in a closer business relationship.

An almost lost art is that of sending thank-you notes for social occasions. A well-written thank-you note still warms the heart of someone who has put enormous work into preparing some event, and you will earn their affection. Some people carry personalized postcards and postcard stamps in their scheduling books so that they can whip out personal notes wherever they are.

HOW TO REMEMBER NAMES

Several years ago I was embarrassed at how easily I forgot names. I could be teaching a class, meeting people at a party, or speaking on the phone, and I'd forget what's his name's name halfway through my first sentence. I knew that Dale Carnegie was right when he said that the sweetest sound in the world is the sound of one's own name. Success with people depends on caring for people, and they can't be sure you care about them until you get their name right. I decided to fix the problem with my own method. Here's what you can do.

Importance: I decided if anything was going to work I would first have to determine how important name recall would be. Using the concept of the "vital few" and the "trivial many," I selected the times when it was most important to remember names. This sounds a bit confusing—isn't it important all the time? The answer is no. Until name recall becomes a natural reflex, you'll have to pick and choose the right times to practice the techniques I'm suggesting. It takes work and concentration. Select the vital few occasions when it will make the most difference, and then give it your full effort.

Description: This step is to have people "describe" their name. I make sure they speak clearly and even spell it. If it's a unique name, I ask for more information and different versions or nicknames.

Repetition: Repeating the name out loud lets you practice saying it and hearing it an additional time.

Quick Usage: Say something...say anything that includes their name. I'll ask a question, make a comment, or just repeat the name again, and tell them that it's to help me remember.

Match: Here's what may help the most. I try to quickly match their name to another person I already know. If his name is "Ed" I might quickly flash on my gymnastics coach, who has the same name. The name "Barbara" may send me to the White House for a quick instant. The point is that next time you see the new person, you'll think of someone familiar whose name you already know.

Ask Again: When I mess up and forget the new name, I've found that the amount of embarrassment correlates with how long I've waited to ask for the name again. The earlier the better.

Get Crazy: Some names are way out there. I try sounding the name out and matching the sounds with everyday objects. "Mohammed" might send you "mowing under a hammock." If I meet a "Harry" and can't think of another "Harry" for the memory association, I'll look at his beard, mustache, hairline, even eyebrows, while repeating the name to myself.

LISTEN: READ MY LIPS!

The importance of listening skills has been discovered lately, and groups ranging from elementary schools to billion-dollar corporations are teaching people how to listen to someone else. Good listening skills and habits can leverage results—from grades for six-year-olds to profits for major institutions.

People have wonderful ideas, stories, and insights, but they may not present these valuable gems coherently. In fact, sometimes it's nearly impossible to extract the essentials from all the other stuff. The ability to sort out the important information in these situations is one thing that separates high achievers from everyone else. Here are a few principles of good listening to help you on your road to achievement.

1. Theme. Start by identifying the main idea or theme of the conversation. When this is unclear, everything else will be confused. It may mean asking the speaker for clarification.

2. Questions. Even if you got the main point all neatly packaged, a few well-chosen questions will clear up details and show the other party that you were listening and are interested in what they're saying. Use their name from time to time to show that you are focusing on them.

3. Paraphrasing. This means repeating the main points, using different words, examples, or analogies. Your brain races about four times faster than the spoken word, and paraphrasing helps you stay focused and also gives you a chance to verify that you really understand the idea.

4. Supports. Attempt to find supporting arguments or links that connect to the main point. These can be arguments for or against the main theme, or they can be key players or events in the story. To explain the entire process of active listening, I use the example of a table as the main theme of a conversation. The supporting details can be thought of as the legs that support the table. Most tables need four legs for support. Active listening uses the extra brainpower to seek these structures out and put them in place.

For example, the "tabletop" active listening technique could be used as you talk to a friend or colleague who is describing a problem at work. As you listen for the main theme (tabletop), you find that the essence of the problem is that she can't say no to new projects. Your questions and paraphrasing reveal two projects that she feels are breaking her back (two supporting legs of the table), and one individual who makes things worse (leg number three), and a kind-hearted soul who makes life at work bearable (leg number four). Your excellent listening keeps you involved, alert, and aware of the essential points being covered.

5. Body Language. Good listening is more than what's going on in your head—the person speaking also gets messages from what you're doing while you listen. Good listening means that most of the time your mouth is closed, and you maintain comfortable eye contact. Avoid excessive fidgeting, tapping, or other distracting body movements.

NETWORKING, PROSPECTING, AND SELLING

Whether you are selling chips, stocks, or yourself, professional networking has been called the new way of doing business. People get together and exchange names, cards, leads, referrals, and anything that might help others in their careers. Good networking includes developing a large database of contacts, asking contacts for leads, finding out what others need, and matching what others need to what is in your database. A workable goal is to follow up on leads or information within 72 hours.

A problem that crops up among new business people and new networking groups is that the difference between networking and actually selling gets muddled. The line between prospecting for good leads and qualified buyers and actually making the sales presentation gets blurred. Successful people know that there is a time to collect information and a time to do something about it.

A good sales course makes a distinction between prospecting for possibilities and closing the sale. Networking helps you get to the right person, while selling is filling the needs of that right person. The time between networking and closing a sale may be months or it may be minutes.

Reaching the right person may be easier than you think. Studies have shown that any transaction can make a complete loop around the nation in 2.7 movements. This means that you can reach any person in the country with fewer than three referrals. John Naisbitt, author of *Megatrends,* claims he can do it with one movement or phone call.

People skills involve learning a sense of timing. In sales, you would avoid attempting to close a sale when the prospect has just had a major catastrophe in his or her life, because they're unlikely to give your product or service much attention. Or in corporate life, if you want to ask someone for support for your project, you might want to make your proposal when they've just succeeded at something, not when they're two days away from a vital deadline on their own project. Your skill and tact with people will help you determine the right time to approach them.

REAL PEOPLE SKILLS

The essence of having great people skills comes from being committed to what you do and interested in what others do. If you have a burning commitment to family, business, or avocation, you will come across with excitement and sincerity on those subjects.

People love to be pumped up and excited about things. An excited speaker can take even a topic you thought was boring and have you sitting on the edge of your seat for hours. You may remember making an investment or going on a trip because someone got excited about a particular opportunity or fun spot. Their excitement rubbed off and hopefully paid off.

143

Most people can spot insincerity. It may take a while, but over time and in different situations the fake will be exposed. People who aren't genuinely interested in others are those who always forget your name, seldom return your calls, and do all the talking.

Taking an interest in the other person guarantees rapport and good conversation. Getting people to really reveal themselves is a skill that can be learned. One way to get someone going is to ask open-ended questions that can't be answered with a yes or no. This gives the other person room to talk about what excites them. The most difficult part may be to keep quiet and let them talk.

You may notice yourself falling into the habit of rehearsing your autobiography while the other person is talking. You may think you can listen and rehearse what *you're* going to say at the same time, because your brain can handle about four times as much information as the person is giving you. However, your face and responses will reveal that they don't have your total attention. Use the tabletop process to help yourself concentrate.

Remember that skilled listening uses your extra brain power to analyze and organize what is being said. When you do this, you will be able to paraphrase or repeat back what they said, thus showing your attention and interest.

People fall in love, literally and figuratively, with those dear souls who take time to show genuine interest in the ideas, dreams, and frustrations of their fellow human beings.

When you give your time and your consideration to the people around you, that genuine interest in others will translate into good relationships. Every human being has a story to tell, a need to fill, and a talent to share. Those of us who listen will discover the talents and interests of other people. This makes living and working with them more fun, and this extra knowledge also allows you to get much more done with less effort. People skills make an enormous difference, not only in how much you accomplish, but in your enjoyment of your accomplishment.

YOUR PUBLIC IMAGE

You may be called upon from time to time to do public speaking or to represent your workgroup or company to clients or at professional meetings. This requires a high level of skill, but most of us don't have the advantage of having been trained as a public speaker, or of professional coaching in our image presentation. We were educated and groomed for other functions.

Nevertheless, for you to be successful at what you do, you need to pass on your skills, information, and conviction to others on these public occasions. The way you present yourself to your clients, customers, co-workers, and investors can make or break your career. Here are five key areas in which you should evaluate yourself and your public presentation.

Speech. The way you talk reveals an amazing amount of information about your training, education, and current social status. In the space of three sentences, your listeners can tell whether you wield absolute power or whether you can't figure your own life out. Everything that pops out of your mouth paints a picture of your past history and future plans. Powerful people tend to think before they speak and quickly summarize down to the essentials. They won't bore you with unnecessary details or waste your time with trivia—they are concise and give you the key points. Only when the main point is made do they move on to present supporting detail.

Body Language. Your eyes, hands, smile, and breathing tell more about you than the words you say. Your listeners learn about your product, your services, and you personally by watching whether you stand with self-confidence or slouch defensively. Be aware of the professional image you're conveying, and make your nonverbal behavior match the quality of what you have to offer.

Appearance. I'm convinced that clean and neat come before sharp and high-fashion. There is no excuse for looking rumpled, in need of a haircut, and with run-down heels and unpolished shoes—no matter what your budget is, you can present a cared-for look. The "dress-for-success" look promoted a few years back doesn't work for everyone—if you're in a creative career, it may be too stuffy, or if you're in an informal industry, it may look too pretentious. Success with people requires that you are always well-groomed and that you dress *appropriately*.

Sincerity. Everyone can spot a phony. If you don't believe in yourself or your organization, you'll have a terrible time convincing others of anything. Sincerity comes from being well prepared and letting your personality and convictions show through.

Zeal. The French use the verb *acharner*, which means to have a powerful drive or commitment to a cause. It's something that fires you up, pumps your blood, and makes you charismatic. You can't manufacture zeal, but you can emphasize aspects of yourself, your services, and your organization that you are enthusiastic about. These are the areas in which you will be able to show *acharner*.

When you present yourself, your services, or your company, people are watching your every move and making judgments about your speech, body language, appearance, sincerity, and zeal. For good people relations and for your public image, keep these things in mind:

1. Be prepared.
2. Be professional.
3. Be yourself.
4. Be aware.
5. Be flexible.
6. Know your audience.
7. Know yourself.
8. Know your topic.
9. Ask questions.
10. Ask more questions.

ARE YOU A GOOD LEADER?

In the book *The Tao of Leadership* (pronounced Dow), John Heider writes: "A good reputation naturally arises from doing good work. But if you try to cherish your reputation, if you try to preserve it, you lose the freedom and honesty necessary for further development." So what is good leadership? Is it something you are, or something you do? Are you born with it, or do you get it somewhere?

Heider seems to think you can learn to lead. He suggests that you:
- Learn to lead in a nourishing manner.
- Learn to lead without being possesive.
- Learn to be helpful without taking the credit.
- Learn to lead without coercion.

Do your leadership skills stack up? Here are some areas to consider in assessing your talents as a current or future leader:

Helicopter Quality. I read an article about the Shell Group's leader selection program. They identified what they called the "helicopter quality" that led to success in leadership positions. They found that men and women who could rise above the clouds and see the broad picture were the best leaders. This quality keeps you calm during a crisis and unbiased with emotional issues. The "helicopter quality" requires excellent communication, a clear understanding of strategy and a balanced long-term outlook.

Self-Preparation. Your education, training, and ongoing reading program give the basics for leadership success or failure. Education and training give you the expertise in your field. A rigorous reading program is a must for all leaders. Most successful leaders devour one or two books a month, along with several magazines and newspapers. An initial benefit of all three is that you gain the skills to do the right things. The second is the confidence you get knowing that your leadership is based on sound footing. Many leaders succeed without extensive education or training. Their leadership may be outstanding but might even get better with professional instruction.

Fact Gathering. As Sherlock Holmes says, gather the facts, put the facts together and *then* make conclusions. The respect and admiration willfully given to effective leaders comes in part from trusting them to do their homework. They consistently take the time and effort to sift out the facts. If a leader gets the facts wrong, even a few times, people will find someone else to follow.

Intuition. After self-preparation and fact gathering, the good leader feels comfortable using hunches, intuition, or plain old "gut feel." The surprise is that a prepared person's intition is as good as an unqualified person's detailed analysis. Intuition turns out to be a subtle mixture of preparation, education, experience, and even the "helicopter quality." Listening skills have a direct impact on intuition. If you can improve your listening habits and observational skills, your conscious and subconscious mind can make better "gut feel" judgments.

Yes, you can be successful in leading people, if you focus on those being led. Heider says it well: "The wise leader is not collecting a string of successes, the leader is helping others to find their own success. There is plenty to go around. Sharing success with others is very successful."

FOR FURTHER READING

Bramson, Robert. *Coping with Difficult People.* New York: Ballantine, 1982.

Branden, Nathaniel. *How to Raise Your Self-Esteem: The Proven Action-Oriented Approach to Greater Self-Respect and Self-Confidence.* New York: Bantam Books, 1987.

Bone, Diane. *The Business of Listening: A Practical Guide to Effective Listening.* Los Altos, CA: Crisp Publications, 1988.

Decker, Bert. *The Art of Communicating: Achieving Interpersonal Impact in Business.* Los Altos, CA: Crisp Publications, 1988.

Heider, John. *The Tao of Leadership: Strategies for a New Age.* New York: Bantam Books, 1986.

Korda, Michael. *Success! How Every Man and Woman Can Achieve It.* New York: Ballantine Books, 1977.

POINTS TO REMEMBER/THINGS TO DO

1. Successful relations with people will help your career.
2. Successful relations with people will help your exercise program.
3. Successful relations with people will lower your stress level.
4. Successful relations with people will help your professional balance.
5. People who remember names are respected, listened to, and rewarded.
6. Attending to interpersonal relations gets as much done as overworking, disciplining, and complaining.
7. Few people can *fake* a sincere interest in others and get away with it.
8. Get interested and enthusiastic about other people's ideas, interests, and goals.

9. In your next several conversations, listen to everything the other person is saying without thinking and planning what you will say next.
10. Focus on what excites and motivates the other person *before* covering what excites and motivates you.

MY PEOPLE SKILLS INVENTORY

_____ I almost always enjoy being around people.

_____ I like meeting new and different people.

_____ I usually remember names well.

_____ I get really interested in other people's ideas, opinions and

concerns.

_____ Parties rarely, if ever, make me uncomfortable.

_____ I usually eat lunch or dinner with others.

_____ I can give bad news reasonably well.

_____ I can accept bad news reasonably well.

_____ I give constructive criticism in a way that's usually accepted

by the other person.

_____ I take constructive criticism so that it's easy to give it to me.

_____ I regularly call people to just say hi and see how they are

doing.

_____ I get along with people of different races.

_____ I get along with individuals who have a different religion.

_____ I do fine with people from other countries.

_____ I tend to like people and they tend to like me.

11

TO FAIL OR NOT TO FAIL

Thomas Edison obtained 1,093 patents. Few people know that this great inventor had hundreds of rock-bottom failures. He invented a perpetual cigar and concrete furniture, but they never quite caught on. He invested and lost most of his fortune in a milling venture, and he wrongly believed that DC (direct current) would win out over AC (alternating current); George Westinghouse won that debate in the marketplace. Rowland Macy had failed at four businesses by the age of 36. On the first day Macy's opened its doors, he took in only $11.06—but things got better! Pick out almost any famous person you admire: you probably know more about their successes than their failures. But if you read their biographies, most of the ones who made it big missed the mark on several occasions.

IS WINNING EVERYTHING?

The place of failure in balanced achievement is poorly understood, and we usually avoid dealing with it, even at the cost of never achieving our potential. In most cultures, taboo topics are seldom discussed in private and never openly mentioned. In our culture, failure is a taboo subject.

Little boys and girls are taught that to be socially accepted, it's important to win in sports and get good grades. As we grow older, these cultural norms become firmly entrenched as the only acceptable adult behavior patterns. Winning in sports translates into winning in everything we do within or outside of our chosen professions. Getting a good report card turns into doing well in high-visibility work and volunteer assignments. We're still as hungry for social acceptance as we were when we were kids.

When we study the history of new ventures—both those that made it and those that didn't, there are four areas of decision-making that seem to affect the outcome of the project: selection of the opportunity to pursue, laying the groundwork for acting on the opportunity, allocation of resources as the project gets under way, and projection of return on investment of resources.

One approach to these four critical areas leads to the ultimate collapse of the project: I call this the success-versus-failure approach. This chapter is designed to shift your approach to risk-taking from a success-versus-failure dichotomy to a change strategy that analyzes the small failures along the way and makes adjustments that lead to the success of the project. But first let's explore the effect of our socialization as kids on our thinking about failure.

HIDING FAILURE

If we always win in sports, get good grades, and have lots of friends, we develop a confident attitude about life but an incomplete understanding of failure. This is actually a handicap, because our inexperience leads us to fear failure, avoid it, and when it happens, hide it as soon as possible.

We see this every day in the newspapers. When large organizations fall miserably short of their sales or profitability goals, the company spokesperson beats around the bush, citing stories of other company successes and providing incomplete data on the current trouble spot.

This reticence to acknowledge failure anywhere in our vicinity shows up in politics, when the family history of many politicians is often cruelly exploited by opponents. Instead of saying that Uncle Joe blew it, the unfortunate office-seeker often sidesteps the accusation, leaving room for their constituents to wonder whether the politician really means that Uncle Joe's malfeasance is okay with him.

Balanced achievement calls for honesty, strategy, and planning. In developing your Careerstyle, these three concepts play an important role in making the decisions that lead you to fail or not to fail.

154

FOUR STEPS TO LARGE-SCALE FAILURE

Analysis of failed undertakings shows that there are four steps that lead to failure: picking the wrong opportunity, acting too quickly, committing resources too early or in the wrong areas, and overestimating the financial returns. Edison and Macy probably went through these phases in many of their ventures. Here is a look at four distinct parts of the process of missing the mark. All four can appear to be perfectly in line with a good achievement lifestyle. A closer look explodes the myth and points out exactly why they almost always lead to frustration and disappointment.

1. Picking the Wrong Opportunity. There's nothing wrong with taking advantage of opportunities. Opportunities to make it big are everywhere. You can invent a new device, sell insurance, invest in real estate, buy hot stocks, coordinate megabuck deals, or start your own business. People make millions in every one of these areas. The problem is that for every one who hits that million-dollar mark there are a hundred who failed and are too embarrassed to talk about it. They saw an opportunity, but it wasn't the right one for their temperament, their attitudes, and their personal goals. Starting out in the wrong area for you personally is a sure way to fail. Make a quick change to another endeavor that better suits you.

2. Acting Too Quickly. We all know that the big winners act on their dreams. Instead of sitting around and daydreaming, winners get out and do something. The real scoop is that by acting alone and without support structures, you are bound to spin your wheels and run out of time, patience, and money. The failure-prone dreamers (and we all know someone who goes off on project after project without one success) tend to substitute activity—any activity—for good contingency planning, networking, strategizing, and evaluation.

These action-oriented types wonder why others move so slowly and do all types of unrelated groundwork instead of tackling the project head on. By quickly acting on the opportunity they make phenomenal progress that impresses friends, investors, and colleagues. Acting quickly on the once-in-a-lifetime deal takes advantage of the high morale, adrenalin surge, and public support connected with new projects, but the truth is that the ultimate success of the project depends on much more than these.

Take the time to lay the groundwork for your opportunity, outline the steps involved, and get some expert feedback on what you plan to do.

3. Poor Allocation of Resources. The third step in the failure process is related to committing resources to the opportunity. Deciding how to use limited resources is always difficult. The time, money, and energy we give to one part of the project is then unavailable for other goals. Nothing will succeed without the proper resources, but neither will it succeed if we commit too many of the wrong resources too early.

I had a failure in introducing a new product, and my primary mistake was in allocating resources. I knew that new product introduction involves developing the product itself, packaging it, promoting it, and distributing it. By overspending on development, buying too much of the wrong advertising, and spending too much time writing the instruction manual, I skimped on the test marketing phase. It was a business productivity product, so I could easily have tested it with my other programs for free, benefited from credible word-of-mouth advertising, and introduced a much better initial version for a fraction of the cost. My problem was that I committed too many resources much too early. Sometimes it's good to be strapped for resources and pressed for time at this stage of a project.

4. Overestimating Returns. The final mistake leading to broken dreams is that of grossly overestimating the speed, amount, and reliability of the return you'll get on your investment of time and money. Let's start with the time it takes for you to make a profit, land that job, get a degree, or achieve financial security. Most of us are amazed at just how long it takes to get our reward. Women and minorities get especially frustrated with achievement delays, because they can't tell whether they're normal career stalls or a result of discrimination. The frustration we have with the slowness of rewards probably accounts for the tremendous market there is for motivational tapes and lectures that assure us that perseverance and persistence will eventually pay off.

When it comes to how much money we expect to get back on our investment, we humans tend to lean toward the high side of pay raises, billings, revenue, or just plain generosity from others. We expect to hit the high side of our sales projections. We overestimate how many customers will pay their bills and how high a raise our boss plans to give us. The funny thing is that even when we have plenty of data, we continue to refuse to calibrate our expectations, and the next time around—by George, they did it to us again!

Finally, we tend to overestimate the reliability of our success. When we get good results, we expect them to continue or improve. In fact, high performance is very difficult to maintain. Social scientists and statisticians describe a phenomenon called regression toward the mean; it describes the likelihood that out-of-the-ordinary behavior is usually followed by more normal or average behavior.

You can probably think of examples in your own life: times when you put in an outstanding performance in sales or athletics, only to have a mediocre or more normal performance the next time around. On the other hand, how many times have you really blown it, only to find that before you have time to work on improvement you naturally improve. All are examples of regression toward the mean. People are complex and so is achievement. Without a solid foundation, our returns are so unpredictable that we end up being overextended and engineer our own failure. It's a good idea to plan for unpredictable variability in what you expect to receive for your efforts.

SUCCESS-VERSUS-FAILURE STRATEGY

The success-versus-failure kind of thinking behind these four mistakes leaves little room for one of the mightiest forces in all achievement: adaptability. Adaptability to new conditions and circumstances eliminates the overemphasis on failure. Continual change and how you deal with it will determine whether your goals end up on the scrap heap or you become the first at the finish line.

157

Let's take a look at the same four areas of decision-making to discover the approach that leads to success through using a change strategy. Approaching your undertaking with a change strategy means that you build your strategy block by block—and each block is a lesson learned or a way you have changed and adapted from some earlier "failure."

CHANGE STRATEGY

Now we're going to take a look at how to use the change strategy to build a solid success. The subtle points in the four parts of the change strategy all work together to gradually build the kind of success we want—and equally important, the type that others will respect and pay for, whether it's to see us perform, buy our services and products, or hire us for our skills.

This strategy is based on the power and pervasiveness of continual change. Whenever we try something new, we're bound to be slightly off target. Like going to the moon, Mars, or Venus, we aim in the general direction and continually make adjustments. The aim is to know exactly where you are going, build the support structure to provide resources, and to anticipate and almost welcome change. With this kind of thinking, ultimate failure is impossible. What we once thought of as missing the mark now becomes an obvious, tested clue as to where the treasure is buried.

I'll never forget the few years I studied classical guitar. My progress was great while I took lessons overseas, but when I returned, something strange happened. As I became more accomplished, I received a steady stream of requests to play at weddings, university programs, talent shows, and church services. I replaced practicing my scales, finger exercises, and other music fundamentals with preparation for each performance. Without the basics, each performance became a nerve-wracking success/failure embarrassment. I hated it and quit when I went away to graduate school. I still have the guitar, but I can't pick it up without thinking success vs. failure in completing a classical piece.

Good musicians know music theory, their instruments, and perform-ance basics. This allows them to make quick corrections that go unnoticed by most of the audience. In other words, when they screw up, they can make subtle, effortless changes in the performance to keep the rhythm and timing of the piece.

1. PINPOINTING STRATEGIC OPPORTUNITIES

The first step is to develop a blueprint of your basic strategy. Look at potential opportunities in the context of your Careerstyle strategy. You know that balanced accomplishment is a result of many things, including your mental and physical health, your goals, your stress level, what you eat, your sex life, and your use of the achievement factors. Now that a goal or project is staring you in the face, put it into perspective by comparing it to your personal and unique way of achieving.

If you have created a strategy of balanced achievement for yourself, everything you do plays to your strengths and improves on your weak-nesses. Ask yourself up front: How does this opportunity fit into my plan of attack? In the beginning, most ideas and projects are vague and unclear, but by comparing them to your blueprint you can more easily pinpoint where they might fit in. For example, when you're giving a presentation, answering tough questions, or are under attack in some way, take a deep breath and bounce the issue off the backdrop of your opinions, principles, and attitudes. This reflective pause will help you see the issue clearly and respond like a professional.

If you have already created or completed your Careerstyle while reading this book, then any additional opportunity can be plugged into the system with little disruption, because you already have a consis-tent, coherent set of objectives that you're living by. Look at the new opportunity like you would look at a job candidate. Anyone who is in a position to hire people knows that if they can get someone who already fits into the culture and has the basic job skills, they will save the organization countless dollars, hours, and repeat recruitment efforts.

Remember that this change strategy is built on making use of mini-failures, and the closer the project or opportunity is to your basic strategy, the better you can quickly use the mini-failures to get you going on the high road.

2. ACTING WITHIN RESOURCES

While a project is getting under way and before you have made the initial changes in direction or strategy, most of your investment of resources will be wasted. Whether it is finding a job, writing a book, or building a space station, it is okay to go second class for a while. The amount of time and money poured into half-baked projects is shameful. People print up useless resumes on exquisite paper, write books on the wrong topic to the wrong audience, and sink educational and social funds into billion-dollar boondoggles. We may need good resumes, important books, and space exploration, but we get better outcomes by acting within current resources and making modifications based on the initial results.

Consider an initial test marketing of your proposal before you jump in with both feet. It is amazing how many astounding ideas surface, even with heavy constraints placed on resources such as time, energy, and money. One of my productivity products deals with group problem solving. Even with a strict 60-minute time limit on the process, groups end up with as many good solutions as when we used to spend four-hour blocks of time on similar company problems.

Remember the hit song "Don't Worry, Be Happy" by Bobby McFerrin? He says the idea came to him in the shower and the lyrics were finished in the studio while he recorded it. Apparently elaborate resources aren't always a must for a successful effort.

How often have you heard people bubbling over about some idea that "can't lose," a product that "sells itself," or a way to make so much money you couldn't spend it all? After all the activity and many upset investors, family members, and friends, I seldom hear about steady positive progress. Instead of controlled and deliberate achievement toward specific milestones, we often hear that things are just "moving along." It is usually the old success-versus-failure syndrome. We want to show quick success to everyone we bragged to earlier. I am personally more impressed and confident when I hear about systematically getting over hurdles and setting up a process that will make things run smoothly over the long haul. There are too many "can't lose" propositions that do lose.

3. DEVELOP A RESOURCE STREAM

You have a vast fund of resources, although you may not be recognizing them as such. Your resources include money, friends, associates, acquaintances, equipment, information, and credibility. All of these and dozens more should form a stream of resources that buttress and support your efforts. As you press onward and bump into stone walls, your resource stream will be in place and ready to get you back on track.

You should begin by rubbing shoulders with lots of people in the field. An even better plan is to actively help some of these acquaintances along with their projects. Your crisis time will seldom coincide with theirs, and if you actively help out you can only benefit by solidifying your stream of resources.

While you master the area you are proposing to enter, the casual observer may think you have flipped as you work on seemingly nonrelated and trivial activities. Be patient: you may not see the payoff for months or even years, but the principle will work.

At this stage the opportunity should get the time and money that it needs and no more. If you use resources for anything nonessential, you are stacking the deck against your success. Develop alternate sources of income and maintain them even when it seems you are past the failure point. Until success is established, low overhead and staying lean allow you to make more changes and modifications so that your project is complete and solid and represents your best efforts.

161

4. DAILY EVALUATIONS

The fourth and final phase of the change strategy is an ongoing process. Each day should include some type of evaluation of the progress and mini-failures. Remember that mini-failures are actually opportunities for breakthroughs if you use them as building blocks in an educational process. The daily evaluations will keep you on your toes about your strategy and any changes you may not otherwise notice. Missing a daily evaluation is not disastrous, as long as you don't miss several and let a real failure begin to sneak up on you.

After you evaluate your project daily for a while, you will discover that your resources are in line and you have turned little failures into some awesome sailing. Without being pessimistic, use your ongoing evaluation to slightly underestimate your rewards and paybacks. At the same time, overestimate the expense, time, and effort you will need. This is not a bad attitude—it's simply common sense.

WINNERS LOSE 70% OF THE TIME

Specialists have found that winners have about a 70% losing rate. Somewhere along the line they got used to losing and know how to recover. Did these people have problems winning in sports, getting good grades, and being accepted socially as youngsters? Sure they did! My feeling is that they learned about this taboo subject at an early age and went on to challenge society in such a way that they transcended their fear of failure. Anyone who can lose over and over again must have some inside information about the future. They seem to know it is a long-distance race and each failure is just a lap around the track. They seem to already know about Achievement Factor #6, M2-LP: More Mistakes—Last Place.

Since you are a human being, and since you are willing to take risks in order to achieve your goals, you're going to have plenty of failures of all sizes. All you need is a resilient and positive attitude based on a plan. Look at the plan, make adjustments, and continue. The plan is key. It must be sound and it must be constantly reviewed.

LAUGH AT FAILURE

Think back to your past and recall what you termed failures. Were they really failures or stepping-stones? You may find that it was your attitude that made the difference. If you labeled it a failure, it was. If you learned and adjusted as a result of your bad experience, then you can't call it a true failure. Use your hindsight for today's and tomorrow's activities, and you'll be surprised at your new attitude.

Ask anyone who has started or managed a business. If they have been at it for more than five years, they'll have some great stories to tell. The more successful they are today, the more they can laugh at the mistakes of yesterday. My feeling is that this ability to laugh and move ahead is part of the reason they made it, and not just an after-effect of success.

THE QUESTION AGAIN?

To fail or not to fail? It's not even a fair question. It depends on you and which strategy you use to run your life. You can continue betting on which side the coin will land on—heads for success and tails for failure, in which case you'll almost certainly have to deal with the question of potential failure. However, if you choose the change strategy and take it slow at first, you can skip this question and head to the gym, the bank, or the golf course.

FOR FURTHER READING

Anderson, Walter. *The Greatest Risk of All: Why Some People Take Chances That Change Their Lives—And Why You Can, Too.* Boston: Houghton Mifflin, 1988.

Jeffers, Susan. *Feel the Fear, and Do It Anyway.* New York: Ballantine Books, 1987.

Viorst, Judith. *Necessary Losses: The Loves, Illusions, Dependencies, and Impossible Expectations That All of Us Have to Give Up in Order to Grow.* New York: Fawcett, 1986.

POINTS TO REMEMBER/THINGS TO DO

1. Washington, Lincoln, and Kennedy had major failures in their lives.
2. Failure can be either a *limitation* or a *stepping-stone*.
3. If you've never failed, you haven't extended yourself far enough.
4. Winners lose 70% of the time!
5. Worrying is usually more painful than the actual event.
6. Figure out ways to eliminate the *embarrassment* from the *failure*.
7. Read three biographies of famous people, and notice how they dealt with failure in their lives.
8. A lost tennis match can be a failure or the roadmap to success.

MY FAILURE CONSEQUENCE INVENTORY

FAILURE (Describe)
Where I Goofed

CONSEQUENCE (Describe)
What Happened Afterward

SOMETHING FROM:

Childhood _____   _____

Teenage Years _____   _____

School _____   _____

Past Job _____   _____

Current Job _____   _____

Family Situation _____   _____

Dating Relationship _____   _____

Sports/Athletics _____   _____

Other Failures _____   _____

MY FAILURE CONSEQUENCE INVENTORY
(continued)

WHICH FAILURE SEEMED TO BE THE WORST WHEN IT HAPPENED?

WHICH ONES MADE YOU GROW THE MOST?

LOOKING BACK, WERE THEY ALL SO BAD AFTER ALL?

12

SETTING THE RIGHT KINDS OF GOALS

One year my school buddy Jean-Pierre and I set a goal to hitchhike from southern France to Rome, Italy. For two hours we stood on the road as hundreds of cars passed us by. Two minutes before giving up, we finally got a short ride with a man who thought the road was a battlefield. What an experience! After a hundred yards we knew the guy was crazy and we might not live to see another stop sign. He passed other cars by using the center line as a passing lane. He seemed to think that the center line was his no matter how many trucks were coming in the other direction. After a full day, we had traveled fifty miles, and at a little town called "Finale," my friend said "Screw this" (in muttered French or Italian), and took a train back to his home.

I pressed on into the night and ended up sleeping in an abandoned boat on a beach in Savona where someone tried to rob me during the night. A day later I made it to the Leaning Tower of Pisa, and after two seconds of thought, decided maybe Rome was too far away to be worth this madness. In two days I had done one afternoon's worth of traveling. My goal suddenly changed from making it to Rome to getting back to my friend's house alive. The nightmare experience continued on the way back. My first ride was a long one, so I slept in the back seat. I woke to find one of the passengers rifling through my backpack. It didn't much matter because my money had run out long before.

I was, by now, tired, scared, and hungry, but the next ride was quite different. The next person to offer me a ride took one look at me and gave me several hundred Italian lira, even though we did not understand each other's language. This got me back to that small town called Finale, where, like my friend Jean-Pierre, I then took a train home. Today I think back and wonder what my goals really were on that trip. Was Rome the real objective, or was it adventure? Could a few minutes of goal setting have made either goal safer and more attainable?

GOOD GOAL SETTING

Let's take a look at goal setting and at the problems that often crop up when it is done ineffectively. The principle behind all goal setting is efficiency—accomplishing objectives more effectively, faster, and more fully. Good goal setting always links the long-term horizon to day-to-day activities. In other words, everything you do during each moment of the day ties into your overall plans in some way.

You may think that this is much too dry and sterile—that if everything you do today has to relate to your goals, you won't have any fun or free time. Remember that in the context of balanced achievement, goal setting means that the goals you set will span every aspect of your work, play, sex, recreation, and growth.

Above-average accomplishment doesn't just happen by itself, nor does it maintain itself. The most powerful way to excel is to make the link between major milestones and individual minutes of the day. Good goal setting is based on the idea that the little things you do all lead up to great accomplishments.

Today's information on nutrition, for example, strongly suggests that what we eat and when we eat it will eventually affect our performance in our career, our business, and our fitness programs.

You may find it disturbing that other people seem to be able to eat junk at any hour of the day or night and still sometimes outperform you. The issue is complex and involves heredity, talent, training, and motivation. You can risk playing on the freeway for just so long. The long-term effect will be performance that will not maintain itself at an optimum level.

Good goal setting allows us to build a framework for lasting perform-ance. By strategically setting goals in different areas that will eventually play off of each other, we set the stage for powerful leverage, because we're using each part of our lives to assist other parts. Translated to the daily level, this means keeping fit, mentally alert, professionally up to speed, and socially/sexually fulfilled while maintaining a solid support system. The best goal setting puts you in a position to keep this delicate achievement balance in full view and on track. All of the Achievement Factors support this balance.

PROBLEMS WITH GOAL SETTING

To some of you, this chapter will be a breath of fresh air and confirmation that what you are doing is right—congratulations! To other people, goal setting may be repulsive. Three possibilities may account for this reaction. First, you may have had a very negative experience (see the chapter on failure), a time when you set a goal, expended tremendous amounts of energy, time, and money, only to see it end up in failure and embarrassment. No one wants to repeat an experience like this.

A second possibility is fear of the unknown. You may think that if you set goals you will not have control of the outcome and thus risk the possibility of promising to do something that you cannot make hap-pen—another very unpleasant situation.

Third, some people know how to set effective goals, but they simply hate to do it. They have experienced the success that goes with setting strategic long-term objectives and then back-tracking into intermediate and then daily priorities. But like many entrepreneurs, they manage to succeed fantastically well with plans on napkins and policies in their hip pockets. Some in this third category continue to make it, and others lose it all.

We honestly don't know all the reasons this third group can succeed without good goal-setting. We do know, however, that goals that are complex, critical, or high priority cannot be completely realized without being tackled in sequential, step-by-step segments. Most of us cannot afford to waste time, money, and other resources as we pursue our life objectives. Whatever hesitation you may have in terms of goals, objectives, or milestones can be overcome with some experimenting and custom tailoring to suit your preference. If you always shoot from the hip, be prepared to have holes in your shoes.

ADAPTING TO CHANGE

Other problems people encounter with goal setting is that they often omit the most powerful determinant of successful accomplishment of any goal, and that is adaptability to change. By getting too involved with the process of setting goals, we sometimes depend on fancy notebooks and elaborate systems. When we get too preoccupied with the details of the process, we may miss the big shifts in what's needed, and it can be hard to change when conditions merit a tactical adjustment or a fundamental movement in a strategy. We would all be less resistant to change if we had a built-in method of continually watching out for change and adjusting for it.

CARROTS AND STICKS FOR REINFORCEMENT

One of the biggest problems people have with managing their goal-setting programs is setting up the consequence or reward that follows the successful completion of the goal. Everybody has a mixture of successes and failures in their progress toward meeting goals, so is it more productive to punish the failures, or reward the successes? Or both?

We are a punishment-oriented society. Giving rewards at the end and even at various milestones is either foreign to many or poorly administered. In the early part of this century when scientific management was in its heyday, it was thought that brute force, careful monitoring, and stern warnings would get the best results from people. This approach assumed that people were lazy and would take every opportunity to cut corners and do less. The terms used to describe this thinking are *soldiering,* the *one best way,* and *Taylorism,* after the founder of the scientific management movement, Frederick Taylor.

Not only does this negative approach still exist today in some businesses, but many of us have turned this thinking inward on ourselves. We call ourselves names, degrade our achievements, and ridicule our own failures. In short, we are to some degree programmed to sabotage our goal-setting efforts by punishing ourselves rather than rewarding ourselves. Study after study in the behavioral sciences field has shown that appropriate rewards for performance have a significant advantage over punishment. Punishment tends to change short-term behavior, whereas a reward-based program achieves long-term results by motivating and teaching. Another problem that many of us have with goal setting is that we lack the patience for the planning and periodic review of our goals. We find it easier to keep in action, trudging along making bits and pieces of progress without reference to milestones and dates for completion. However, when we attach a date to a milestone or an overall goal, it reinforces our commitment and some of the ambiguity is removed. The patience to plan and wait is something many would-be achievers either don't have or refuse to exercise. If that's the case in your goal setting, simply set a date for something and work toward it. Review your progress by counting it down by days or weeks, and then reward yourself for each small increment of progress.

Remember to remain flexible. Your goals are for *you,* personally, and not the other way around. Change whatever parts are outdated or just plain mistaken. This flexibility will make the next round of goal setting less painful or scary.

WHEN NOT TO SET GOALS

Never set someone else's goals or objectives. This is primarily for those who have some sort of supervisory control over others. The worst thing you can do for morale and teamwork is to dictate what others will accomplish. By depriving them of the process of setting goals, you effectively remove them from ownership of the goals you've set.

Ownership of any goal, objective, or milestone draws upon forces that are poorly understood but visibly effective in their accomplishment.

It is also a very bad practice to set a goal that takes the credit, or even appears to do so, from another person or group. The classic example is in a bureaucratic organization where two people or groups converge on one goal. Conflict occurs when both parties take credit to the exclusion of the other. It is much better to declare the objective as a joint effort or specify the part that each one will accomplish. A group effort should not be claimed as a personal goal.

THE F-A-C-E METHOD OF DECISION MAKING

My work in problem solving and decision making has led to an interesting finding. After deciding to make a decision or tackle a problem, most individuals and groups want to quickly get to the final stage. As tempting as it is to move quickly to completion, it is important not to bypass critical steps in the process. The first solution is rarely the best.

I have taught what I call the F-A-C-E decision-making process for several years, and it has a good application in goal setting as well. During the heat of battle, beleaguered managers can always remember F-A-C-E:

> F: Gather the FACTS.
> A: Analyze the ALTERNATIVES.
> C: CHOOSE and implement.
> E: EVALUATE the results.

In workshops and on-site consulting I find that the tendency is to short-circuit the process and jump to the choose-and-implement phase, while the evaluation is often left out altogether. Goal setting should not take place until you reach the third (choose and implement) step. If you do it sooner, there is a high probability that your goals will have to be redone. You need to analyze your goals in view of your overall strategy to see how different alternatives might fit in. Time taken to gather facts and analyze alternative choices will usually pay off handsomely.

An example may help. A 35-year-old professional woman feels she is not moving ahead in her job as rapidly as her male co-workers. She gathers the FACTS and finds that yes, male co-workers with identical experience have been promoted after about 2.5 years, and that after 3 years she hasn't moved at all. Her ALTERNATIVES are to wait another six months, try to transfer, or seek a job outside the company. Let's say she CHOOSES to go for the internal transfer. That is precisely the time to start the goal-setting process, not before. She can now decide where the company is heading, which department best fits her Careerstyle, and how to subdivide her ultimate objective of an internal transfer into bite-sized chunks or daily activities. Her Careerstyle plan will also help her maintain balance between her personal and professional life during this transition.

HOW TO SET GOALS

All goals should be based on the purpose of your career, business, or personal development program. By starting with the big picture you can be sure that each goal or objective fits into your strategy for high achievement. In addition to being strategically tailored, goals must be specific, realistic, measurable, and with a timeframe or due date. A few examples will describe what I mean.

EXAMPLE 1: CAREER

Purpose: To advance steadily in my chosen career while building financial security and professional respectability.

Goal: To find a new job in my field that pays 10% more than my current salary within the next six months.

Is this goal specific? Yes. This goal clearly states what type of job at what pay scale is needed. It also specifies a similar field.

Is this goal realistic? Depending on the person and economic conditions, yes this is probably realistic. This usually carries a subjective evaluation.

Is this goal measurable? Yes. Easily measurable at end of six months.

Timeframe: Six months from the date the goal is being set.

EXAMPLE 2: BUSINESS

Purpose: To eventually create and run my own business based on my lifestyle, interests, and abilities.

Goal: By the end of next month I will identify three different types of businesses I could start and run successfully.

Is this goal specific? The goal is very clearly spelled out for this stage.

Is this goal realistic? Yes. It's not unreasonable.

Is this goal measurable? Each selection or option must be one that fits into the overall purpose behind this person's career change.

Timeframe: End of next month.

EXAMPLE 3: HEALTH AND FITNESS

Purpose: To maintain a lifestyle that keeps me fit and healthy for as long as I live.

Goal: My goal is to do two types of outdoor (aerobic) exercises totaling four workouts a week. Each will last at least half an hour and I will start this week.

Is this goal specific? Yes, it's spelled out very well without vague and ambiguous terms.

Is this goal realistic? Maybe, as long as they are not jumping from zero workouts to four and provided they have no medical problems.

Is this goal measurable? There is no problem counting the number of total sessions as long as two different kinds are included each week.

Timeframe: It might be better to plan a gradual increase up to this level over four to six weeks. If the person is already in a workout program, this timeframe is fine.

EXAMPLE 4: ROMANCE

Purpose: To upgrade the satisfaction in my love/romantic life.

Goal: To have one full day a month where my partner and I experience new things and learn to communicate better. We'll start next month.

Is this goal specific? It's okay, but the "new things" sound a little vague. Something specific like traveling, dining, or sports activities would make it more specific.

Is this goal realistic? Sure, as long as the partner is willing to participate.

Is this goal measurable? No problem here.

Timeframe: Starting next month.

SUPERB GOALS

I list these final points under superb goals because they give you the edge that makes regular goals naturally build momentum and gain support from other influential people. Good politicians and good salespeople tie their ideas and products to the heartbeat of their communities and customers, and superb goal setters also link their goals to the flag, motherhood, and apple pie. As we mentioned in

Chapter 4, there are regular kinds of goal schedulers and those who fall into the expert category. Here are some ideas that put polish on already good goals.

LEVERAGE

Our definition of leverage is the strategic management of inputs and resources to achieve maximum outcomes and results. We have already discussed how to use leverage in many areas of achievement. With leverage you get more accomplishment with the same or less activity. Now, just like politicians and salespeople, you can use current hot topics to boost your efforts toward success. You can tie your goals into current trends and attitudes for an extra bit of leverage. Current trends and changing attitudes are already doing some of the work, and the more you leverage this free labor, the more each of your small steps will result in giant strides toward your goals.

For example, take a couple in their late thirties that decide to slow down on their career push and finally start a family. They decide to leverage their goal of having two children within five years with the growing trend of corporate day-care centers. They know that good leverage means power to be effective, so they decide to write articles, open a center, and lobby local companies to open more day-care centers. The positive outcomes are that they become knowledgeable parents, their new lifestyle automatically includes time with the kids, and they protect some of their future income that would have been spent on expensive child care. All of these benefits result from tying their goals into a national trend toward corporate child-care centers.

IMPORTANCE TO MANKIND

There is a certain natural pull in most people toward doing something for humankind. Legacies are made by linking your goals to movements or developments that have an effect on the lives of large numbers of human beings. Politicians, television evangelists, and even terrorists tie their causes to the fabric of many people's lives. If your goal will benefit all men and women in some way, you have already enlisted the help of thousands.

This is not to suggest that you bend the truth in any way, but if somewhere in your program there is a positive and real benefit to others, you're one up on the competition. It may take a lot of work to publicize the connection, but if you can show that your goals are linked to a broader good, you have an advantage. Examples include teaching public speaking, counseling troubled kids, or writing about cholesterol reduction benefits.

CONVERGING INEVITABILITY

Without going to a psychic or having inside information, we often see trends that are moving powerfully in some direction. Two recent examples are fitness in the workplace and the negative effects of women imitating male workaholic lifestyles. These two trends suggest that companies will incorporate more fitness programs and women will suffer more of the traditional male ailments in the future. Many individuals and organizations are setting goals based on their degree of confidence in the inevitability of prevailing trends. Market researchers spend thousands of dollars to find which trends are converging.

A number of businesses linked their goals to their belief that there was a distinct group of Young Urban Professionals (YUPPIES) who were making more money and starting to have babies at a later age than was formerly true. These businesses made fortunes on products and services aimed at this perceived group. As you build your Careerstyle goals, try to identify as many related trends as possible, and structure your goals to take advantage of the trend's inevitability. Look for trends that are productive and constructive, or identify ways to take advantage of negative trends by heading them off or reducing their side effects.

MAKE OTHERS SUCCESSFUL

A fitting conclusion to a chapter on goals might suggest that you stay focused on what you want without letting others distract you. Quite the opposite. Sure, we all need to stay focused, but for your balanced achievement to be successful, your focus should be expanded to include other people's goals, successes, and priorities. The more your goals make others successful, the more you've succeeded in stacking the deck in your favor.

No one will support you for very long if they see little return or gratitude for that support. The thrill of reaching your goals will begin to turn sour if your focus is too narrow and does not include the success of others. It's worth the effort to take regular goal setting and turn it into superb goal setting by enlarging your focus to include other people. You can do this whether your goals include foreign travel, a new business, or better relationships.

By the way, the next time I decide to go to Rome, my first step will be to book transportation. That is, of course, if my goal is to get there in a reasonable amount of time. If my goal is adventure, I may still fly to Rome instead of hitchhiking, but the objective of the trip will be much clearer and I will probably get a lot more done with much less effort and risk.

FOR FURTHER READING

Alberti, Robert, and Michael Emmons. *Your Perfect Right: A Guide to Assertive Living.* San Luis Obispo, CA: Impact Publishers, 1988.

Ellis, Albert, and William Knaus. *Overcoming Procrastination: How to Think and Act Rationally in Spite of Life's Inevitable Hassles.* New York: New American Library, 1977.

Lloyd, Sam. *Developing Positive Assertiveness: Practical Techniques for Personal Success.* Los Altos, CA: Crisp Publications, 1988.

Winston, Stephanie. *Getting Organized: The Easy Way to Put Your Life in Order.* New York: Warner Books, 1978.

Winston, Stephanie. *The Organized Executive: New Ways to Manage Time, Paper, and People.* New York: Warner Books, 1983.

POINTS TO REMEMBER/THINGS TO DO

1. Set professional and personal goals.
2. Use a goal-setting system that fits your own style and preferences.
3. You will accomplish *twice as many* of your goals if they are written.
4. You will accomplish *three times as many* of your goals if they are publicly displayed.
5. Those who help others succeed are more successful themselves.
6. Try chipping away at large projects rather than tackling huge amounts.
7. Reward yourself whenever you accomplish a written goal.
8. Little rewards (breaks, small purchases, a movie, a special meal out, or a mental "Way to go!") have as much effect as some of the major rewards (a vacation, car, or boat).

MY GOAL INVENTORY

PROFESSIONAL	PERSONAL

MAIN GOAL_____ MAIN GOAL_____

PARTS OF A MAIN GOAL   **PARTS OF A MAIN GOAL**

A.   A.
B.   B.
C.   C.
D.   D.

OTHER GOALS   **OTHER GOALS**

1.   1.

2.   2.

3.   3.

4.   4.

5.   5.

6.   6.

7.   7.

8.   8.

PROFESSIONAL GOALS Summary   **PERSONAL GOALS Summary**
"What I'm trying to accomplish"   "What I'm trying to accomplish"

_____   _____

_____   _____

_____   _____

_____   _____

_____   _____

13

THE PSYCHOLOGY
OF ACHIEVEMENT

This chapter takes a broad and practical look at the field
of psychology and how it relates to balanced achievement. It is
not intended to be an in-depth academic review of psychological
concepts, but rather a brief overview that allows you to take a
critical look at what psychologists have discovered. These
concepts may seem to be pure theory to you, but if you digest
and apply these next few pages, you will understand
yourself better and have some tools that allow you
to control your own behavior.

SCHOOLS OF THOUGHT

This entire book has dealt with aligning our behavior into
strategic patterns that set the stage for balanced accomplishment.
The intent of the field of psychology is to study, predict, and
modify human behavior.

The classical schools of psychology include structuralism/
introspection, functionalism, psychoanalysis, humanistic
(personality and gestalt), and behaviorism. In a sense, each of these
general areas has specific ways of studying personality, learning,
and motivation.

Some areas of psychology aim more directly at balanced
achievement than others, and those were the specialties chosen for
this chapter: learning, personality, and motivation. You'll get a
glimpse of what psychology says about these areas, as well as a
look at Abraham Maslow's hierarchy of needs and the 15
characteristics of the self-actualized individual.

LEARNING

Psychologists who specialize in the psychology of learning study the best and most efficient ways of acquiring and using new knowledge. They say that most of the process of learning is simply making connections between events. Learning is divided into the stages of acquisition, retention, and recall or demonstration. First you have to receive the information, then you store it, and later bring it back for use. Learning is usually measured by its quantity, speed, or accuracy. You can see that learning and achievement are close cousins. Although learning can occur without much application, the actual implementation is an essential part of achievement.

Learning is usually defined as relatively permanent changes in behavior based on past experience. In a broader definition, this includes changes in personality, attitudes, and beliefs that are distinct from past experiences and perceptions. The successful professional looks at learning as a tool that can be understood, refined, and applied toward their personal strategy of high achievement; basically, you can find better ways to teach yourself new "tricks." If you pick the right tricks to learn, you can get better results at work, in business, or with your body.

At the risk of getting too dry for some and not specific enough for others, we will review some of the key elements of learning research, tying it to principles that you can apply in your own Careerstyle.

CONDITIONING DOGS WITH BELLS AND FOOD

Pavlov is commonly known for his work on behavioral conditioning with dogs. He showed us that by training dogs to associate bells with food, he could use the bell to get the same reaction as the food itself. Many television commercials take advantage of this principle, showing, for example, vivid food images that people associate with satisfaction of hunger, then associating those images with a product to create the expectation of satisfying food. This is *classical conditioning*, which focuses on automatic responses without much thinking involved. *Operant conditioning,* on the other hand, requires that the subject of the study actually do something before there is a reward or punishment.

Operant conditioning says that the person must act and the consequences of that action determine whether that behavior will happen again. B. F. Skinner pioneered much of this work and stressed the distinction between responding after something happens (classical conditioning) and operating before something happens (operant conditioning). Conditioning or learning takes place in both cases. The term *conditioning* consistently refers to strengthening the ties between a stimulus and a response. Sometimes the stimulus comes before the response, like when we jump at the sound of a loud noise or become sexually aroused by the smell of perfume. Other times the response comes before the stimulus, as when we put money in a vending machine and wait for the package to drop or when we make a romantic pass and are accepted or rebuffed.

The term *reinforcement* describes the process of influencing behavior with either positive or negative consequences. In the next few paragraphs we will take a closer look at the laws that govern the reinforcement of activities. *Extinction* is a term that refers to the elimination of behavior due to the lack of reinforcement. Patterns or schedules of reinforcement have been extensively studied to determine how to use rewards to teach, maintain, or extinguish behaviors. In general, the findings have shown that steady, continuous rewards quickly get the behavior going, but as soon as the reward stops, so does the behavior. However, if the reward is variable and is not given every time the behavior occurs, the behavior continues when rewards stop and is extinguished very slowly.

HOW WE LEARN

There are three laws generally connected with the psychology of learning that support much of what you have read in earlier chapters. They are the Law of Effect, the Law of Exercise, and the Law of

Frequency. Each one states in profound yet simple terms that, other things being equal, human learning can be predictable and manageable. In other words, your ability to balance your life can be learned and well organized. Let's take a look at these three laws.

LAW OF EFFECT

This law states that any activity will be strengthened if surrounded by satisfying events or weakened if surrounded by annoying events. The relationship to Careerstyle, exercise, nutrition, and success in general is clear. We can engineer our environments in ways that foster doing the right things.

Half the battle, of course, is to figure out what the right things are. Psychologists refer to this dilemma as a "figure-ground" issue. This refers to the phenomenon that people with different learning histories differ in their accuracy in distinguishing correct images from a confusing or "noisy" background. You may have seen those pictures with the "hidden" person or plant. Some people see the objects immediately, while others can't make them out until someone outlines them with a pencil. As soon as they say, "Oh yeah, now I see it," it becomes a figure instead of background.

The important parts of life are usually mixed in with the background and our job is to make them become more figure and less ground. Only then can we begin to make something of the important parts that we select. You'll recall that the principles of good goal setting suggest that you first separate the important from the trivial (figure versus ground), and then set goals. You can manage your life better by surrounding the useful activities with satisfying and pleasant circumstances.

LAW OF EXERCISE

Believe it or not, the Law of Exercise came from the psychologists long before the focus on fitness hit every commercial and cereal box. This law states that the repetition of any activity promotes learning and makes the next performance easier. This is a principle that goes way beyond physical fitness or career development. The Law of Exercise says that repetition can make it simple to build good habits when we include it in our lifestyles.

This law is another way of saying that practice makes perfect, or in the improved version used by many athletic trainers and music teachers, "Perfect practice makes perfect." Pick what you want to be good at—or get paid for—and then do it often and do it right.

LAW OF FREQUENCY

The Law of Frequency relates to the acquisition of a new activity. It says that if you increase the repetition of an activity or an association (swing racket—hit ball), it will lead to a more rapid acquisition of that skill. There's definitely some overlap with the other two laws, but it does suggest that we can increase the speed of learning, or as we say, "move up the learning curve," to reach standard or above-average performance more quickly. Here again, as with the figure/ground dilemma, we run up against first deciding what we need to learn and then marshaling all our forces to learn it properly, adequately, and quickly.

PERSONALITY

Among psychologists, there is a lot of disagreement about where our personalities come from and whether they are predictable. For example, are men born to be emotionally strong, while women are predisposed to be sensitive? And how about our other beliefs and stereotypes? Do you believe that accountants and engineers tend to be loners and do not care much for social company? Are entrepreneurs risk-taking high achievers who ran neighborhood lemonade stands as youngsters? All of these statements refer to various ways we think of ourselves and those around us, and to describe something we call personality.

Some psychologists believe that we are born with strong tendencies that will form our personalities. Others insist that the first few years of life develop our personalities just as a photographer exposes a roll of film and then develops it into a permanent picture. Another school of thought says that no matter what we are born with and whatever happened while we still had baby teeth, our personalities are formed by current events and circumstances.

WHOLES, SUMS, AND PARTS

Why is personality research important to the successful professional? Gestalt theorists are famous for demonstrating that "the whole is greater than the sum of its parts." Even if you analyze all the individual parts of a situation or someone's personality, you will never get the complete picture until you view the subject as a whole entity. The whole takes on an entirely unique meaning. The psychology of personality studies the whole person in its quest for an understanding of human behavior.

This area of psychology stresses that we humans thrive on having a purpose for action. It gives us credit for being able to choose the types of results we want, how we will go about getting those results, and the way we will respond when we get them.

CONSCIOUS AND UNCONSCIOUS LEVELS

Conscious thought is a central theme in many of the humanistic areas of psychology. Although the unconscious drives formed by our heredity and childhood experiences influence us, our ability to think and reason is an equally powerful force. If this were not true, there would be no need for a book on balanced achievement because your conscious powers would be useless. For normal, healthy people, conscious thought is the primary driving force and the area that should receive most of their attention. In the treatment of abnormal behavior, of course, unconscious patterns should be explored insofar as they can assist in bringing the person closer to a normal range of behavior.

Careerstyle is built on your ability to effectively get the right things done in the right amount of time. Its foundations include planning, balance, strategy, success, and health. Because unconscious forces are those that you are unaware of or that you cannot naturally bring to the conscious level, you will do well to leave them to the experts and focus on more tangible areas that you can easily influence. There is convincing evidence that the degree to which you entertain your positive or negative thoughts and what you say about your life can affect the subconscious. When you say a thing, some part of your mind believes it. People with healthy personalities tend to say and believe positive and uplifting things about themselves. This is healthy nourishment for the subconcious.

STUDYING THE WHOLE PERSON

Personality is often defined as traits that are organized in a unique manner. Each of us has bits and pieces of shyness, honesty, suspicion, thriftiness, laziness, creativity, and drive. You could define personality as the combined proportion to which we have each characteristic. This combination also determines what we will be predisposed to do in any given situation.

The other part of the equation is the outside world, which can be very reinforcing or very unforgiving. This combination of our personality traits and the consequences of interacting in a dynamic world molds our personalities. It is this combination that gives human beings unique personalities that are somewhat constant over a wide range of behaviors. This is why much of the work on personality studies the whole person in the setting of his or her environmental surroundings.

A final note on personality: our perception of our world and its events may be more important than the physical events themselves. In other words, it is our beliefs or interpretations about what we experience that influence us, not the events themselves. This explains the fact that brothers in nearly identical settings can turn out to be almost opposites in tastes, opinions, and career accomplishments. One may be a senator while the other does ten years in prison. Or two girls grow up together and go to the same college and law school, but one ends up on Wall Street while the other chases ambulances or airline disaster victims.

The psychology of achievement suggests that you can manage your perceptions of your experience in such a way that you launch a successful career and lifestyle rather than languish under someone's else's oppressive thumb. The psychology of achievement is geared to convince you that you can create an environment, designed to meet your mental, physical, and social needs, that supports you in creating the Careerstyle you choose.

You're now in the final full chapter of this book, and you should have gathered by now that you have the tools and resources to engineer your own learning and personality development. Now we enter the realm of lighting a fire under your hindquarters to get you into action!

MOTIVATION AND MATCHES

Motivation is the match that lights that fire under your seat. In order for us to move into action, we sometimes need a little flicker and other times we need a blow torch, but in either case, we need the match to get the fire started.

The most common view is that motivation is the result of biological or psychological deprivation. We can be deprived of food, water, sex, air, or friends. As the length of deprivation increases, most of us engage in activities that will yield whatever is being withheld. If mental or physical pain is involved, we take action to reduce that pain.

Many behavioral psychologists take an opposite view of motivation. Their research suggests that the behavior comes first and is either reinforced, extinguished, or punished. Their view is that a person is motivated by recalling the past histories of the behavior and the consequences that followed it. Both views are useful for the successful professional.

THOUGHTS CAN MOTIVATE
HIGH ACHIEVEMENT

High achievement comes from a harmonious set of actions aimed at a properly defined goal. Something must motivate the high achiever to perform the set of actions even before tasting the fruits of success. The high achiever may receive secondhand or vicarious reinforcement. He or she may be simply modeling the types of behaviors of a respected mentor or may have imagined the positive consequences out of the clear blue sky. Remember, perception is key—if you think it, then it is almost real.

The professional who practices Careerstyle finds motivation to get achievement started or learns from past experiences which activities tend to be rewarding and then does more of them. Deprivation of something desired can motivate, as can the presence of something painful. It is obvious that pain will make you jump and deprivation of something important will make you take action, but what about that pain between your ears that is not a headache?

PAIN BETWEEN THE EARS

Cognitive dissonance is a mental type of motivator. Leon Festinger, who originated the concept, noticed that people selectively gather information that supports their views and may not even notice observable facts that disprove their opinion. When we have to deal with opposing evidence or beliefs, we are said to experience *dissonance.* Our selective editing serves to reduce dissonance in our minds.

For example, after we buy a car we tend to find more evidence that we made a superior choice, while skipping over any evidence that we got nailed to the wall. We do not like to hold two ideas in our mind that contradict each other.

Another example is that of someone who publicly speaks out in favor or a project or plan. Until that point, they may not have been completely in favor of this viewpoint, but after speaking out, they become almost fanatically committed. Speaking up and then *not* supporting the idea would create dissonance.

When this dissonance occurs we usually modify one idea or somehow bridge the gap between them. This pain between the ears can be a strong motivator in a negative way. Research says that we all experience this cognitive dissonance, but we seldom recognize our sneaky ways of reducing it. Mature individuals recognize this dangerous possibility and will be open to criticism from others. If negative or questionable feedback comes from several sources over a period of time, watch out! You may have been lighting the wrong fire! Listen and then be ready to make some honest changes; this will save a lot of aspirin! I recall being told that I was a little too defensive in taking criticism. My automatic response was, "No I'm not!"

MASLOW AND CAREERSTYLE

One of the most famous models for motivation was proposed by Abraham Maslow in his Hierarchy of Needs. He proposed that human needs are filled in a step-by-step fashion, and that we are not motivated to deal with more sophisticated needs until all the basic needs—those lower on the hierarchy—are fulfilled. He listed as the most basic needs those of being physiologically warm and well fed, and of being physically safe. When these needs are handled, we can deal with our social, belonging, and esteem needs.

At the top of Maslow's pyramid are the self-actualization needs. It is interesting to compare Maslow's description of self-actualized personalities to see how closely they mirror our concept of Careerstyle. Here are Maslow's fifteen characteristics of the self-actualized person:

1. Clear perception of reality
2. Self-acceptance
3. Spontaneity in thought and behavior
4. Problem-centered rather than ego-centered
5. Need for privacy

6. Independent of culture and environment
7. Appreciates basic life experiences
8. Mystic experiences
9. Social interest
10. Satisfying interpersonal relationships
11. Democratic attitudes
12. Enjoys the means as well as the ends
13. Sense of humor
14. Highly creative
15. Resistant to enculturation

These are not necessarily goals to shoot for, but rather simply characteristics of people who regularly fall into the top level of Maslow's pyramid of needs.

TWO TYPES OF MOTIVATION

There are two types of motivation. First is the type aimed at gaining success. This motivation is characterized by realistic goals and achievable milestones to be accomplished along the way. Mature healthy achievers design their sources of motivation to fit into this category.

The second type of motivation is fear of losing. Some people are obsessed with avoiding failure. The motivation to avoid failure is characterized by goals that are either too high or too low and by milestones that are too easy. In a sense, these high goals are the excuse for failure, whereas low goals and milestones help avoid embarrassment because they are easily reached.

WRAPPING IT UP

The psychology of achievement is a useful addition to our introduction to Careerstyle. This final chapter was intended to educate, stimulate, and bother you just a bit. You should come away with a healthy understanding of your own psychological make-up and how you have control over your own beautiful and unique Professional Balance.

Your success in lifelong satisfaction and achievement depends on the quality of the overall plan and your rigor in sticking to it. You now have the foundation to begin working.

My fingers are crossed, hoping that you have constructed a Careerstyle that is a powerhouse of strategy, broad based and evenly balanced. Your vigor, alertness, and effectiveness are influenced by your thoughts, habits, diet, and exercise. Every goal you reach carries a slight imprint of your balance in work, play, sex, and treatment of other people. Although you can never control everything that influences your life, you have absolute control over the important things. You alone make the day-to-day decisions that keep you honest in following your Careerstyle or that allow you to stray into unproductive territory. Now that you have constructed your plan, it will be the little decisions that decide how well you do. Make each choice count.

FOR FURTHER READING

Benson, Herbert, and William Proctor. *Your Maximum Mind: Change Your Life by Changing the Way You Think.* New York: Random House, 1987.

Bliss, Edwin. *Getting Things Done: The ABC's of Time Management.* New York: Charles Scribner's Sons, 1976.

Bone, Diane, and Rick Griggs. *Quality at Work: A Personal Guide to Professional Standards.* Los Altos, CA: Crisp Publications, 1989.

Johnson, Spencer. *The Precious Present.* New York: Doubleday, 1984.

Lakein, Alan. *How to Get Control of Your Time and Your Life.* New York: David McKay, 1976.

POINTS TO REMEMBER/THINGS TO DO

1. Psychologists have much to say about how we learn things and what makes us keep doing what we should or should not do.
2. Learning relates to somewhat permanent changes in our behavior.
3. List two to three things you disliked at first, but learned to enjoy later (such as beer, eggplant, girls, boys...).
4. Each of us is conditioned by certain sights, sounds, smells, and topics.
5. The *more* you do something, the more it becomes a *permanent* part of your life.
6. The *less* you do something, the more it will begin to *fade*.
7. Your personality is somewhat permanent, but you can learn to change parts of it.
8. Your thoughts can directly affect how you feel, how you see things, and how you act.
9. Compare your own balanced lifestyle to Maslow's 15 characteristics of the self-actualized person.
10. Read *Professional Balance* more than once.

MY ACHIEVEMENT INVENTORY

Circle = Past Goals   Square = Present Goals   NA = Not Applicable

YOUR ACHIEVEMENT   % PERCENT COMPLETED

YOUR ACHIEVEMENT											
Educational Plans	0	10	20	30	40	50	60	70	80	90	100
Family Plans	0	10	20	30	40	50	60	70	80	90	100
Financial Plans	0	10	20	30	40	50	60	70	80	90	100
Health/Fitness Plans	0	10	20	30	40	50	60	70	80	90	100
Weight Control	0	10	20	30	40	50	60	70	80	90	100
Career Plans	0	10	20	30	40	50	60	70	80	90	100
Hobbies/Skills	0	10	20	30	40	50	60	70	80	90	100
Reading Plans	0	10	20	30	40	50	60	70	80	90	100
Writing Plans	0	10	20	30	40	50	60	70	80	90	100
Personal Development	0	10	20	30	40	50	60	70	80	90	100
Charity	0	10	20	30	40	50	60	70	80	90	100
Business Plans	0	10	20	30	40	50	60	70	80	90	100

ADD SOME OF YOUR OWN:

_____	0	10	20	30	40	50	60	70	80	90	100
_____	0	10	20	30	40	50	60	70	80	90	100

YOUR RESULTS!

A. Use one color to connect the circles to see your *past trend* of accomplishment.

B. With a different color, connect the squares to see how you're *currently progressing.*

14

CONCLUSION

Completing the work in this book is more a beginning than a conclusion. You've started on a journey that can be very exciting and productive. You had the initiative to begin the book and the discipline to complete it, and these two characteristics have been instrumental in getting a whole lot done in many lives. Not many people take the initiative to begin a book that's longer or thicker than a magazine. Of those who start, it's the ones with will power or a good system (for example, reading ten to fifteen pages a day) that regularly complete what they start. You are one of the few who have shown the desire for balance and have acted upon your intention.

You can't change your life just by waking up one morning and saying, "I'm going to be a better speaker," "I'm going to weigh less," or "I'm going to be more successful with people." You won't get results simply by wishful thinking. It takes solid information to start with, repetition of new information to really understand it, and constant application of new principles to actually make changes.

It's a 1-2-3 process: (1) input the information, (2) repeat to build understanding, and (3) apply the principles. *Professional Balance* was written to get you moving in all three areas. As for information, this book has given you leads and tips culled from the best information out there. You've been exposed to good introductory material on health, success, achievement, and male-female roles. Your next move should be to follow up with more reading and studying in the areas in which you are weak, which you should have identified when you did each chapter's self-inventory. A good place to start your further investigation would be the books recommended for further reading at the end of each chapter.

Now you have to make sure the ideas are repeated in your mind. Each bit of information you acquire has to compete for shelf space in your mind; if you repeat your reading of this book and review the principles given, the things you want to remember to practice will win out in the competition for long-term memory space. I would suggest that you use a different color of highlighter pen each time you read a chapter. It will help you clarify for yourself just what you're working on at each reading. I would love to have you walk up to me someday and show me your copy of the book with two or three different colors showing your different readings of the book!

Now, as for application: This is where the rubber meets the road. You've got to get up, get out, and do something. You've learned that it doesn't have to be a major undertaking, and it doesn't have to be done perfectly (Achievement Factors 2 and 6). Choose something, anything, to do for 21 days until you have the habit formed. Fool your brain by writing just one sentence, reading two lines, or pedaling five times. Having no time to apply Professional Balance is no excuse. Do a part of it now! Your brain will build the habit. Just a second...okay, I'm back. I just took 40 seconds to write a thank-you note to someone who did me a favor. I'll address and send it later. The important thing is that part of the task got done immediately—no excuses.

Start by applying Careerstyle and Professional Balance to smaller areas of your life, kind of as a test. Careerstyle combines your professional career with healthy lifestyles. Pick two or three simple things that combine these two parts of your life. Eat a salad while you write out some rough goals, or invite a business associate to go jogging or biking with you. Or get together with a trusted boss or co-worker to indulge in a relaxing drink or after-work cigar while you outline career strategies. These combinations of health and relaxation activities with career-enhancing situations sum up Careerstyle. (More about occasional vices later.)

Underlying the concept of Professional Balance is the belief that everything you do can be improved with consistency, variety, and moderation. A balance among all parts of your life—physical, mental, spiritual, social, and professional—will deliver a long and steady stream of achievement and satisfaction in your life. If you are overdoing in one area, experiment with sneaking some time away from it and plugging that time into one of the weaker areas of your life. For example, if you work out too much in the gym, take some of that time and apply it to the professional or spiritual side of your life. If you always work late, reallocate a few of those hours to the physical, mental, or relationship part of your life. Begin with minor changes, just little tests of what you read in this book.

Another area in which to cultivate balance is within each segment of your life. You may be perfectly balanced among the several areas. Your mixture of social, professional, mental, and physical activities may be ideal for your goals and tastes—fantastic! Take a second look within each area and check for equilibrium. Your social life should include close personal contact as well as the party circuit. A well-rounded spiritual life includes communal worship as well as silent, private meditation. Balanced physical fitness does not mean jogging ten miles a day and nothing else. Huge thighs with an emaciated upper body make a poor picture of physical fitness.

Your occasional indulgence in a relaxing vice really *does* fit in. In the big picture of your life, a little spice "ain't gonna hurt nobody." I'd rather see people dip into the cookie jar once in a while than see them become so neurotic and fanatical about perfection that they drive themselves and the people around them crazy. I couldn't prove it, but my gut feeling is that balanced people can thrive while having a couple of vices, provided they do no long-term harm to themselves or others, and provided that they don't set a bad example as a role model. If you set yourself up as a balanced individual without fanatical tendencies, others will place your occasional vice into the perspective of being human. You'll also be more fun to be around.

Balanced living and working come from understanding, and understanding comes from the repetition of the essentials. You should have a good feel for the essentials after reading this book. Go ahead and add a few principles of your own. Start practicing what works for you. Good luck in creating your own Professional Balance!

Appendix

100 WAYS
TO CONTROL STRESS
AND NURTURE SUCCESS

1. Pick positive outcomes. Pick three positive outcomes of any situation you think is stressful. Focus on favorable results instead of the negative ones.

2. Go for a walk. Researchers say a brisk 17-minute walk is as effective as taking a Valium. Extra benefits include better circulation, digestion, and the chance to pick a few roses.

3. Take five deep breaths. Getting oxygen to the brain is a good way to clear up your thinking so you can handle stress. You can do this anywhere and anytime. Be careful not to hyperventilate. If you are making a presentation, make notes on your outline to remind yourself to take a full breath.

4. Stand and stretch. Blood circulation is increased when you stand, stretch, and move about. Your mind and body are quickly rejuvenated and poised to tackle the tough cases.

5. Talk to a friend. Confiding in someone takes the load off your own mind and gives you a new perspective. Remember, a conversation goes two ways. Combine your confiding with listening.

6. Eat a good breakfast. Fighting stress takes ammunition, and breakfast is essential fuel for those who cope well. There is some evidence that your body uses morning calories for energy and stores evening calories as fat. In any case, eat something light to start the day.

7.   Make a fun call. Drop your daily checklist and just make a fun call, but don't spend more than a few dollars. You'll end up in a much different frame of mind.

8.   Work on a pet project. You deserve to spend time on what pleases you. Put everything aside and enjoy yourself for at least half an hour.

9.   Spend time with a pet. Cats, dogs, birds, hamsters, horses, even snakes (for the select few who like them) can work wonders in reducing stress.

10.   Watch an aquarium. The lights, scenery, fish, water, and the "games fish play" are a great diversion that helps you cope. The responsibility of tending to fish helps you focus on something other than your problems.

11.   Close your eyes. Combined with deep breathing, this can help you regain equilibrium. Closing your eyes for as little as 30 seconds can reduce tension. It's better if you can find two to three minutes.

12.   Imagine you're on a beach. It's a beautiful day and you are totally relaxed. Visualize the sights, sounds, and smells you would experience on the beach..

13.   Imagine you're on a mountain. The wind is blowing and you love it. Pictures in books and magazines can improve on this valuable childhood skill.

14.   Pretend you're sailing. Just visualizing yourself skimming across the water is very relaxing and calming.

15.   Leave the car. Walk to a restaurant or deli for lunch. The extra three or four minutes are not as critical as you think.

16.   Leave the car. Take a cab through a congested part of town. A few dollars spent, but a lot of peace of mind gained.

17. Leave the car. Take mass transit every few weeks for a change of scenery and pace. The change of scenery is important, along with the time to do some personal assessment.

18. Buy a bicycle. Go for a fun ride at least once a week. Always wear a helmet. Select routes that are safe and peaceful.

19. Fix the bicycle. Get that old bicycle up to speed. A few dollars or a couple of hours is all it'll take. You'll feel productive as you learn a new skill.

20. Find your bicycle. If it's buried somewhere in storage or in the garage, start digging. Bicycling can be a stress reducer for life...just watch for cars!

21. Cut out sugar. Try it for two weeks—absolutely no added sugar. You should see quite a difference in your stress and alertness levels.

22. Make a daily checklist. Start each morning (or end the evening before) by writing down tasks that need to be done that day. This helps keep you on track when you get distracted.

23. Make a monthly plan. Set down a strategy plan for the month, save it, and review it. Make it useful without becoming a chore. Everything in this plan should come from the annual plan.

24. Make an annual plan. Take some time to organize your year in 12 monthly sections. Don't get bogged down, but rather outline the year's accomplishments, improvements, and positive outcomes (forget the usual January 1 resolutions).

25. Make a five-year plan. It takes work, but it can shed light on what's right and what's wrong in your day-to-day activities. Five-year plans should be revised each year. Keep aiming at your general career goals and the personal things you would like to do.

26. Set reasonable goals. Your goals should be within reach after some effort. Don't play superhero. Don't be lazy.

27. Ask for help. People are waiting to help, but you'll have to take the initiative—unless your friends can read minds!

28. Reward yourself. Loosen up and give yourself a treat, be it ice cream, a movie, a cigar, an album, a new dress, or a nice dinner. Yes, being balanced still allows you to be human and even have a vice or two.

29. Acknowledge yourself. If you are turned off by tangible rewards, just say something nice about what you've done in a way that makes you feel good.

30. Toot your horn. It's been said that "he who tooteth not his own horn getteth not his horn tooted." Whether it's horns or squeaky wheels, men and women need the attention they genuinely deserve.

31. Listen. Others have greater and lesser problems than you. Listen with interest and compassion. Use the extra brain time to get into their story and let your own story go for awhile.

32. Listen. Stop planning what you are going to say next. Get into their story by organizing and analyzing what they're saying.

33. Listen. Other people really do have good solutions. Resist saying "I already tried that." Let people completely explain their idea before judging it.

34. Listen. Young people have novel and innocent ideas that are dynamite. Their ideas can work wonders if we let them.

35. Listen. Older folks have seen it before. They are patient and seldom have a vested interest. Ask and listen to them—and you'll brighten their day too!

36.   Read about stress. Many good books have been written. You will begin to see the same recommendations over and over. Understanding and recognizing your own stress is a good first step toward improvement.

37.   Read biographies. Famous achievers went through hell in their lifetimes. Many died before getting their reward. When you read about Thoreau, Van Gogh, and Mozart, your stress may be more manageable.

38.   Follow leaders. Select leaders in your field and keep track of them. You'll see they have troubles too. Watch how they handle their down times.

39.   Find a real mentor. Get the right person to agree to be your mentor. Be cautious with their time, and use it wisely. Send thank-you notes when they're helpful.

40.   Create a "phantom" mentor. Can't find the ideal mentor? Then make one up. Build you own ideal role model. Don't send thank-you notes!

41.   Write a letter. We all love to get handwritten letters. Make someone smile. Buy "Thank You," "Congratulations," and blank cards. Send one every day!

42.   Grab an apple. Eating fruit instead of pastries, candies, or heavy foods will give you a lift and make it easier to handle stress. Your body will have one less battle to fight.

43.   Try juice. Instead of coffee, substitute one or two cups of juice during the day. Plan to add juice to your shopping list and to the office refrigerator.

44.   Work with plants. Watering, planting, and transplanting have a calming effect. Good solutions come during these calming periods.

45. Call ahead. Call to warn that you may have trouble meeting a financial or any other commitment. People are surprisingly understanding.

46. Make good-faith payments. When you make small payments, the creditor may or may not appreciate it. You will respect yourself for making the effort.

47. Do cash-flow planning. On a sheet of paper, list all dollars coming in and going out. Analyze the balance and plan ahead for the unexpected.

48. Overestimate costs. Most activities will cost more than you think. Build in a 10%-15% buffer to reduce your stress level.

49. Underestimate revenue. Unfortunately what we expect is often more than what we finally get. Plan ahead for less. Keep your optimism and fight for what you deserve, but base your commitments on 10%-15% understated revenue.

50. "Save a shilling." Live by the old adage that if you earn 99 shillings, you never spend more than 98. Live by this rule no matter how much it hurts.

51. Take the day off. Take an occasional day off in the middle of the week. You may feel guilty at first, but it'll go away by about 9:00 a.m.!

52. Leave town. Just for a day or a weekend, surround yourself with some different scenery. No need to spend much, just leave.

53. Take a class. A course in stress management is a valuable investment. Plan to attend every session and read all materials.

54. Take a class. Take a course in something you know nothing about. This should get your mind off the usual activities in your life.

55. Sponsor a kid. Help a kid get ahead in life. Several organizations would love to get a call from you. You'll forget your troubles while doing something extremely productive and rewarding.

56. Sponsor a team. Many youth sports depend on the support of concerned professionals for their existence. You'll feel a definite lift.

57. Visit a museum. Local museums offer a variety of changing programs. A quiet walk-through will educate you while having a calming effect.

58. Admit it. You have a stress problem. Plain and simple, admitting it comes before you can do anything to improve it.

59. Find the source. Track down the source of your major stressors. Where, when, or who do they come from? Write your impressions down on paper to make yourself a little more objective in your analysis.

60. Track the frequency. Write down each time a specific event causes stress in your life. Do this for several days.

61. Assign an intensity. When a specific stressful event occurs, give it a score between 1 and 10 (1 = low, 10 = high). Write it down or make a mental note.

62. Chart the intensity. Track your progress as you try to lower the intensity level of specific stressors. Focus on one or two at a time.

63. Get a massage. Find a reputable masseur/masseuse and take the time to treat yourself. Check the phone book or ask friends.

64. Record the feeling. Get a mental or written fix on how you feel after positive experiences. Remember the feeling when you are stressed.

65. Join a network. Get involved with a formal organization that can pave the way to reaching some of your goals. Actively participate without overdoing it.

66. Diversify your reading. Select a book that is not career related. Read 10-30 pages each day. Read at the same time and in the same place if possible.

67. Diversify your reading. Subscribe to a magazine not related to your field. This will get rid of those feelings that it's your duty to read every word of the magazine before throwing it out. Browse through it, relax, and then toss it.

68. Switch your pattern. Take a different route when going to usual places like work, shopping, or visiting. Being totally predictable is not only boring, but it also saps a lot of vitality. Do something different!

69. Switch the order of your usual pattern of doing things. When the new pattern gets routine, switch again.

70. Change the furnishings around. Move your desk, table, file cabinet, etc., into new places. You may find the new arrangement more practical and refreshing.

71. Find new photographs. Exchange the photos on your desk and walls for up-to-date shots. Take them yourself if you have photographic skills and equipment.

72. Contact school friends. Look up some of the people you knew in school. Surprise them with a call or note, or drop in on them. It's a great feeling to reminisce on the good times you used to share.

73. Contact past co-workers. Find out where they are, what they are doing, and how their family, job, and love life is going. They'll appreciate the contact.

74. Express your fear. Let it out that you are scared to death. Things will immediately feel lighter and less gloomy.

75. Express your love. Others need and want to know that you love them.No need to be a Shakespeare—just say what you feel.

76. Express your anger. Getting mad and holding it in will hurt you. If you blurt it out, it may hurt others. Try expressing it assertively (just between aggressive and passive).

77. Express your concern. Concern for others tends to get repaid when you need it most. It's an investment in your stress reduction.

78. Know your strengths. Having unshakable confidence in your true talents is a major asset in stressful situations. Pull out those congratulation letters, diplomas, and award certificates. You earned them.

79. Know your weaknesses. Ask people for feedback on your weak points. Ask them to be gentle but frank—you need it for improvement. Take notes.

80. Find your "gray areas." Strengths and weaknesses are the extremes; the middle ground is equally important.

81. Explore unknown deficits. Many times we don't know what we don't know. Reading, chatting, browsing, asking, and listening can help clobber the "unknown" unknowns.

82. Attention to detail. The little details will make you a hero or they will kill you. Learn to master them or they will master you. "Do it now" is good advice.

83. One-trial learning. Make sure new information enters your mind correctly the first time. The goal is to eliminate the need for unlearning bad actions and relearning the good ones.

84. Do it right the first time. Take two minutes to avoid a two-hour re-do at a later date. Fifty percent of all effort is wasted in some companies. Don't let it happen to your life. One hour of planning usually saves four hours of activity.

85. Ask an extra question. Even if you know the answer, an extra question may yield more data for better decisions. If you're like me, you'll find you knew less than you thought. The only stupid question is the one not asked.

86. Use expansion questions. Expansion questions go deeper and further than regular "yes/no" questions. More data leads to fewer useless mistakes and less stress. People enjoy expanding on their ideas and dreams.

87. Tap different resources. Think of it as "drinking from a different well." New sources of problem-solving information abound. Go look for them.

88. Learn high technology. The labor- and frustration-saving inventions of the past decade are not as difficult to learn or as expensive as you may think.

89. Use high technology. After learning something new we tend to fall back to comfortable ways of living and working. Push yourself to try the new "toys" until they become second nature.

90. Tackle things head-on. Take the bull by the horns, do difficult tasks first, finish A-priorities before C-priorities and "get down and do it"!

91. Achievement Factor 1. Tailor your activities according to your strengths.

92. Achievement Factor 2. Use the behavioral training effect to build habits into your lifestyle even when you don't have time for the full-blown activity.

93. Achievement Factor 3. The 3-4-5 nutritional rule stands for 3 meals, 4 food groups, and 5 glasses of water (separate from meals).

94. Achievement Factor 4. Run those full-length mental motion pictures. Be sure to play both the "gloom" and the "glory" reels.

95. Achievement Factor 5. Use leverage to get more output per activity. Remember that "one step at a time gets the high achiever nowhere."

96. Achievement Factor 6. Making more mistakes and coming in in last place is not a goal, but the result of progressively moving upward into more challenging situations.

97. Achievement Factor 7. Spacing your diversions—whether they are the withdrawal (vacation) or the substitution (different task) type—can have a great impact on reducing stress.

98. Achievement Factor 8. Hitting the 3-for-1 sales of life eliminates one or two unnecessary trips. Use the time to focus on strategic goals.

99. Achievement Factor 9. Goal scheduling can be learned. The experts have learned it and use it to reduce their stress levels.

100. Achievement Factor 10. Input incubation allows new things to settle. Without it, you run the risk of unnecessary mistakes, wasted time, and lots of back-tracking.